BEYOND WINS

BEYOND WINS

EASTERN MINDSET FOR SUCCESS IN DAILY BUSINESS NEGOTIATIONS

MALA SUBRAMANIAM

LIONCREST
PUBLISHING

*For my parents, Janaki and Veerabhadran,
whose wisdom and compassion are my
inspiration. For my husband, who paved the
way for my career in corporate America.*

CONTENTS

ACKNOWLEDGMENTS

It was during one of my lectures on negotiations when someone in the audience said, "Mala, why not write about this? What you teach would prepare someone for the training programs on techniques for negotiating." That was my inspiration to write this book. I thank my former employers and clients for the experiences that helped my professional development. I owe a big thanks to everyone who attended my speeches, training, and executive coaching.

Frank Taylor and Joan Rothman, the only two people I was proud to call my "boss," inspired me to think beyond my job and make a difference with each of my employers. How can I sufficiently thank my friend and mentor, Laura Cohen, who gives new meaning to optimism? Joan Capua was my first friend in my first job in a bank after getting my MBA. She walked me, a naïve person from India, through the maze of corporate challenges. She took the time to read my manuscript and gave me feedback that inspired confidence in me to move forward. Laura Trisiano is my friend and mentor, guiding me in every step of the publishing process with her creative thinking and inspirational messages.

Authentic folks who took an active interest in my book and gave me honest critique and suggestions for improvement include Randall Whitfield and Macy Whitfield. I want to make special mention of Macy, who did amazing research to give me an overview of other books on negotiation and wrote a five-page critique of the original manuscript. I cannot imagine writing another book without the support of these wonderful people.

The following business leaders, authors, philosophers, and works have influenced my thinking throughout my career.

W. Edwards Deming	J. Krishnamurti
Phillip Crosby	Mahatma Gandhi
Dale Carnegie	HH The Dalai Lama
Steve Jobs	*The GITA—Words of Wisdom*

I derived some rules for success in this book from observing my family members. My father, who dared to dream and succeeded; my mother, a role model for maintaining emotional equilibrium in adversity; and my daughter, Lalitha, and son, Sairam, are my inspiration for this book, and they are proof that intelligence can coexist with humility. The true meaning of a contemplative mindset is found in my brother, Dr. V. Ramanathan, a genius and a pioneer scientist in global warming. I look at dark clouds and worry about rain. He looks to see how they impact humanity and what he can do about it. His research and dedication give meaning to combating fears. He makes me understand that fear is asking, "Oh, what will happen to me? How can I protect myself?" and courage is wondering, "How will it impact others, and what can I do to help?"

Ellie Cole, senior publishing manager of Scribe Media, was my anchor throughout the publishing process, and stood as a pillar I could lean on when I had my bouts of frustration and doubts. Hal Clifford, editor in chief, encouraged me to unlock the Eastern wisdom within me, and put it boldly in print for the benefit of readers.

I strongly recommend everyone read *Getting to Yes: Negotiating Agreement Without Giving In* by Roger Fisher and William L. Ury after you read my book. If you have read *Getting to Yes* already, read it again. Their strategies for negotiating will take on a new meaning.

RIGHT MINDSET
SIGNALS SUCCESS

A man is but the product of his thoughts;
what he thinks, he becomes.

—Mahatma Gandhi

As you begin your journey with me on the road to success in negotiations, you will get the answers to these burning questions: Why do I feel like I am on a seesaw of wins and losses in my business negotiations? Even when I win, I sometimes feel like I lost something. Tools and techniques I picked up in books and training are not foreign to me, so what am I missing? What will put me on the path to success? What is the yardstick for success?

I feel your pain because I have been there. Who in the working or business world is spared the pain or pleasure of negotiating? Everyone negotiates at work to get the job done. No one works in a vacuum. It takes the support of many individuals both within and outside the company to accomplish even simple tasks at work. Most people do not know that they are "negotiating" every day to achieve the goals set for their job.

I started as a market analyst in a large bank in New York City, where I learned the need to negotiate. The job required working with people from many departments within the company, and with vendors for completing major projects. What started there on a smaller scale plays a significant role even today when working with clients to design and deliver training for their employees. There has not been a day without negotiation in twenty-five years of working for employers in diverse industries. My former employers are IBM, GE Healthcare, Dun & Bradstreet, Horizon Blue Cross Blue Shield of New Jersey, and Chase Bank [Manufacturers Hanover Trust]. Getting things done in these companies meant working with multiple departments, and sometimes with people from other parts of the world. The experience gave me a good handle on what works and what does not in day-to-day negotiations.

Since 2007, I have run a workshop titled *Soft, Yet Powerful Negotiations* for corporate employees that manage technical projects for their clients. They are client-facing professionals or account specialists. One of these specialists, who attended my first class on negotiation, complained, "I don't know why I am in this class. I am an engineer, and my role is to implement the billing system for our insurance client. I don't have to negotiate with clients. Our salespeople do that."

These specialists were primarily from the technical field and thought their job was to manage the implementation of automated systems for their clients. They did not realize that daily interactions with clients and internal people in their own companies were exercises in negotiation. How did they handle these interactions? Some complied with client demands. Some said *no*. Others who had a working knowledge of negotiation adopted tactics learned elsewhere but were still uncomfortable with negotiating. They expressed pain points common in business situations, such as the fear of losing a client, alienating a business partner, incurring the anger of peers or management, and last but not least, the potential for financial losses.

A SHIFT IN YOUR MINDSET

Through the associations at work with people from different countries, I learned that a person's *mindset* determines success in any business negotiation. Feedback from the account specialists that attended my training also led me to conclude that these professionals could see better results from conventional strategies and tactics for negotiations taught elsewhere when they experienced a shift in their mindsets.

So, I mix a little Eastern philosophy with US business psychology in this book to create *a shift in your mindset to focus on building long-term business relationships and results.* "I need to work with this individual. We can achieve more if we see value in each other's contribution and focus on long-term mutual benefit," is a powerful thought. Bend the curve and master the shift to attain success at all levels of business negotiations. The ultimate destination in business is the achievement of profit, whether the company is a sole proprietorship, or a small, medium, large, or global company. Regardless of what job you do and whether you know it, you are negotiating every step of the way in your own business or as an employee of a company to contribute to this profit. Every opportunity to negotiate opens the door to build long-term relationships, which pave the way for profit.

You are probably wondering, "What is unique about Eastern philosophy and how can I apply that to solve business problems?" It is about having a Contemplative Mindset that looks beyond today to focus on those actions that may be beneficial in the long run for both sides. Measure success by how many people you take on your journey to accomplish business goals, not by how many people you leave behind as failures because they could not keep pace with your proficiency in arguments.

EASTERN INFLUENCE ON BUSINESS

India is a country in the Eastern Hemisphere and has a significant influence in the region through the *principles found in the ancient teachings of India for everyday life.* Yoga is one such a principle that has several layers and depth beyond modern interpretations. What is more popular is the set of movements and postures, or *àsanà* in hatha yoga, which teaches the method of synchronizing mind, body, and breath. They now offer yoga even in fitness centers throughout the US to create a balance in people that treadmills cannot achieve. It is part of the contemplative mindset that should help a person remain centered in all situations.

Likewise, this book shares a few fundamental principles from the ancient teachings of India to achieve the contemplative mindset for success in negotiations. Most Indians learn these principles at home, schools, and the community, and from the teachings of philosophers.

In this book, Eastern philosophy or mindset refers to the knowledge originating in the ancient teachings of India. The US is in the Western Hemisphere and provides an advanced model for businesses around the world. US business psychology could benefit substantially from the contemplative mindset of Eastern philosophy. These principles help leverage the business acumen of the US to create a balance in daily work situations. This book integrates the essence of these principles, along with practical applications, illustrations, and real-world examples for solving business problems.

SOUND BITES OF THE
CONTEMPLATIVE MINDSET

Here are the sound bites from the ancient teachings of India that have practical applications in the business world:

- *Path to understanding* is a methodical approach to seeking knowledge. The first step in the method is listening with an open mind. Next is recollecting what you heard, going inward to think through what you heard, and validating the information with experts to gain the intelligence. Finally, letting the intelligence shed light or reveal new insights. The Communications Signal described in this book is similar in concept to the *path to understanding* for reaching a shared understanding of the business problem before negotiating.

- *Màyà, a Sanskrit phrase, is a trick of the human mind.* A well-known analogy for this is a person, walking in the dark, who sees a rope at a distance and mistakes it for a snake. Whenever the intellect does not understand something correctly, it projects its interpretations. People see things the way they want to see them or how it is convenient for them. The caution here is to acknowledge one's limitation to see things as they are.

- *People create the world around them.* One's surroundings are not the cause of anyone's problem. How they perceive it is the problem. If they accept that, then the solution is within their reach. If they don't own the problem, they cannot own the solution. When people perceive themselves as the product of external influences, they spend time trying in vain to change their surroundings rather than looking within to see how they can change themselves to be successful in the existing environment.

- *Desires give rise to likes and dislikes.* "I want this; I like this; I don't like that; and I hate that," are the sentiments that come out of people's desires. When desires are not fulfilled, they get angry and disappointed. Anger clouds their judgment. It shuts down their power to discriminate between what is right and what is wrong and distracts them from achieving their goals. Anger makes them react to situations, trying to prove they are right, rather than taking a responsible approach with the intent of solving the problem.

- *Making wise choices.* The choice is between what is transient and what is permanent. In business situations, this concept translates to a choice between wins that don't last and relationships and results that

do. Success is a combination of relationships and
results that last.

- *Ego gives one a sense of identification—you identify
  who you are by the role you play in life or at work.* "I
  am the head of this department" gives one a sense
  of responsibility and power. It is the abandonment
  of responsibility and the attachment to this power
  that causes problems. Fear of losing this power gives
  rise to anger, jealousy, animosity, and other negative
  emotions that lead to conflicts.

- *Fear stands in the way of compassion.* Fear is asking:
  what will happen to me? Courage is asking: what will
  happen to others, and how can I help?

- *Intention [known as "sankalpa" in Sanskrit] is a powerful
  influence in your life.* If your client's success is your
  intention, then you are paving the way for your
  success. Likewise, hopes and dreams create positive
  outcomes for any initiative you undertake.

- *Silence does not mean being quiet or not talking; it is
  our nature.* Silence is a way of creating harmony in
  relationships. Conflict is not between people. It exists
  in our minds based on how we perceive others. Silence
  helps resolve the conflict in our minds.

US business psychology is guided by two principles: *time value of money*, and *to each his own*. This time-orientation and self-reliance drive goals, ambitions, and the processes to achieve rapid results. The businesses give an opportunity for people to speak up, share ideas, and advance in their careers. Companies reward people for their individual contributions. Innovation, research and development, and dreaming big are at the heart of new business growth.

Blending the two, the Indian contemplative mindset and the US business acumen, generates positive results in negotiations and success in business.

THE *CHAKRA* OF NEGOTIATION PRINCIPLES

Chakra is a word from Sanskrit. *Chakra* means "a wheel." The Communications Signal and the Seven Rules in this book are the eight spokes of the *chakra* or wheel of negotiation principles (see Figure 1). This wheel blends the contemplative mindset of Indian philosophy with US business psychology to prepare people for success in their negotiations. The ancient teachings also use the phrase *chakra* to denote the energy centers in the human body. The seven *chakras* are the subtle energy centers in the body, and keeping them balanced promotes good health by maximizing energy flow. Mainstream medicine does not discuss these subtle energies in our bodies. The *chakras* are part of the ancient Indian teachings. Likewise, the principles in this book are subtle and may not be the strategies taught in mainstream negotiation classes. The negotiation *chakra* (wheel) has eight spokes, or centering principles, to balance your mind and energize your negotiations. Put the *chakra* in motion with the eight principles, which include the Communications Signal and the Seven Rules, to create a healthy balance in your business relationships and results. The more you practice, the higher the likelihood that these principles will help reduce anxiety and stress, remove fears, and energize every business interaction.

FIGURE 1. The *Chakra* of Negotiation Principles.

The Communications Signal follows the pattern of the traffic signal and walks everyone through a step-by-step process of understanding the business problem that requires negotiation. The Signal also helps people recognize when to negotiate and what would happen if they started the process prematurely. Wait for the Green Signal to go! It is all in the timing—if you react to client demands rather than working your way to a mutual understanding of the problem, the results would be as harmful as running a red light. You will experience a shift in thinking by learning how to uncover the right problem and how to approach negotiations at the right time. This Communications Signal is the differentiating factor in my teachings—it is the foundation for a contemplative approach to negotiation.

Most negotiations fail if there is no common understanding of the problem. Think of negotiation meetings when both sides are in a heated discussion about a solution. However, there is no agreement on what the problem is. Take a vendor-client situation where the business intelligence report generated by the vendor has several errors. The client thinks the problem is with the analysts assigned to the project by the vendor, and the vendor concludes that the data provided by the client was inaccurate. Both may be right, both may be wrong, or one is correct, and the other is not. The first order of things is to figure out the problem, and not who is at fault.

The Seven Rules are the seven spokes on the *chakra* (wheel) that help ease the way into success in any negotiation.

Employees frequently have the same questions and complaints when working across departments to get work done for clients.

> *Questions:* Why do I feel like I lose every argument with clients, vendors, and other departments in my company? Why is it so difficult to get my work done? I've tried different strategies, but none seem to work.

> *Complaints:* Clients are very demanding. They have no appreciation of the hard work I do and keep piling more work on me. Other departments in my company don't support me in getting the job done. Management does not give me the needed resources to do my job.

Most participants in my classes tried to adopt the strategies gleaned from recommended books and training programs, but their pain persisted. The Seven Rules in this book heal the pain of negotiating by showing that others do not inflict the pain; most of the time, these are self-inflicted wounds. Change your mindset and then negotiation skills, strategies, and tactics become meaningful tools.

ARE YOU READY TO SHIFT YOUR MINDSET?

This book is for people who are new to negotiations or wondering why their approach to negotiations has failed. If people are relatively new to negotiation, they have no built-in bias, so this book infuses the right thoughts to frame their mindsets for success. If they have done negotiations before, they will probably get more out of the book, because they will gain the mindset that will help them better leverage their skills to be effective in daily interactions at work.

Not everyone is a stranger to the Seven Rules in this book, but what brings to life the Seven Rules are the many business examples, stories, and scenarios coupled with the list of questions to ask oneself in different situations and a practical guide to adopting each rule. Most cases relate to client interactions, which are the most challenging in business relationships. If people learn to handle them effectively, the same rules will apply to their other business relationships.

You will appreciate the Four Ps (problem, process, people, and parameter) that govern negotiation strategies and tactics. Negotiations are less challenging if you adjust your business language for people in different departments, such as executive, finance, marketing, and operations, or for people with four distinct working styles characterized as planners, movers and shakers, doers, and talkers.

It is necessary to prevent or prepare for those situations that could derail your negotiations. Cultural differences can throw negotiators off the track. Behaviors and communication styles vary around the globe, and people need to know of the differences and learn to adapt their negotiation styles to each country. One universal style will not lead negotiators to success.

Although it provides definitions of basic business terms relevant for understanding negotiation, the book assumes the reader's familiarity with a few business phrases such as customer needs and expectations. It gives a new set of definitions for such phrases common to the business world as: communication, client, win, and success. The first few chapters in the book include concepts that provide the foundation for creating a change in your mindset before you engage in any business negotiation. You will get a deeper understanding of these concepts with an analogy not heard before in business interactions.

ONE

THE BIG QUESTION

*For success, attitude is equally
as important as ability.*

—Sir Walter Scott

D o you want to win, or do you want to succeed?
Emma was the director of marketing in a large
company. She had to work with the director of sales;
the managers of product development, operations, and information technology; and the marketing vendors to launch
new products. Emma's annual bonus depended on two factors—the timely launch of new products without exceeding
the budget, and customer feedback. She had a track record
of completing projects on time and within the budget. She
had also earned the trust of senior management. She was a

winner! Emma knew how to get coworkers, staff, and vendors to agree to her terms and conditions. Management applauded her method of setting goals and aggressive deadlines, and developing plans and rigid schedules. However, she was not popular with her staff, other departments, or vendors that implemented her projects. The turnover in her team was high. Many quit, found other jobs, or moved to other departments within the company.

Emma had an initial meeting with the managers involved in a new product launch. The managers raised some concerns about the budget, the aggressive deadlines, and her plan. They even told Emma that the vendors were not willing to bid on this project. Emma was not ready to change anything, and the meeting concluded with no resolution. She scheduled another meeting and sent an invite to her staff and the same managers to discuss roles and responsibilities. The meeting invite included an Excel spreadsheet with the details. Her staff had no choice but to attend, but the other managers made excuses for not attending. They said that they had too many demands on their time. Emma escalated the issue to her boss, Ted, who was new to the company. Her former boss had always intervened on her behalf, but Ted had a different approach to work.

He asked Emma a series of questions.

"Why did all the managers refuse to attend? Do they have top priority projects? If they do, where does your project rank in order of priority? If they don't have priority projects, why are they refusing to attend?"

"Why are the vendors declining to bid on your projects? Why do you have to get a new vendor for every project?"

"I also see you have a high turnover in your team. Why? Do you realize that every time an employee quits, the cost of replacing that person is high? You are not saving us money by launching products on time. You have been in this job for a year. How long can you keep up this record of wins, without the willing support of people?"

Emma was so focused on her job priorities, achieving her goals, and getting the bonus check, she had never stopped to think. Emma did not understand Ted's questions. She viewed winning as a positive thing. It's what she was wired to do. She thought, "Ted's line of questioning is not congruent with how winners think."

Ted asked, *"Emma, do you want to win, or do you want to succeed?"*

Winning is short term. It marks a competitive event, with a start and a finish. You set a goal for the event, and if you achieve it, you win. When you win, others lose. You can win a race, a battle, or a competition.

Success is long term. It's a continuous path of building and sustaining strong business relationships and results. Negotiations are essential parts of these relationships. Success does not focus on winning or losing. Success is not about getting the perfect contract that contains all your terms and conditions. It's the value you create along the way so that everyone involved can contribute to the business goals of the company. Negotiation is an opportunity to create a value-added solution, expand your role, and enhance revenue for the client and your company. If people focus on short-term gains in their client projects—wins—they may lose sight of the larger picture of keeping the client and the steady flow of revenue—success.

Your whole mindset changes if you turn your attention to long-term relationships. Is 'yes' in negotiation a milestone or the destination? Yes, no, gains and losses, and win-win are all milestones on the value-path to lasting relationships. For instance, you have a client who changes requirements when the project is nearing completion. You are in a dilemma: do you say yes, do you say no, or do you get the client to say yes to your solution? This book frames the situation as an opportunity to expand your relationship with the client. Build a relationship brick by brick, with each negotiation serving as a brick.

Negotiation is a relationship-driven process to reach an agreement with another person or entity to address a business opportunity or resolve a situation that is causing problems for both sides. Each agreement is a milestone to create, expand, or maintain the business relationship. For people who see negotiation as working on a deal, the final agreement or contract, along with terms and conditions, is the conclusion. So negotiators put the effort into creating these perfect and sometimes airtight agreements. Putting all the effort into the perfect contract is a precursor to failure.

The overarching question throughout the process should be, "Will the terms or conditions in the agreement hurt or help the relationship?"

Unlike bargaining, negotiation is not an event with a start and a finish. What is the difference between bargaining and negotiating? Bargaining is a focus on getting the best deal. It is an event with a start and a finish concluding in a win or a loss. An excellent example of bargaining is buying a car, where both the buyer and dealer worry about making the right deal. An airtight contract matters here. Negotiation is longer term and looks at what is good for the relationship. Responding to a customer's request for changes in an ongoing project would qualify as a negotiation.

Negotiation is in the fabric of every business relationship. If negotiation conjures up a vision of hostile people sitting across the table from each other and debating terms and conditions of a sales or labor union contract, think again. Many situations in companies could give rise to opportunities for negotiation. How about a simple telephone chat between two employees to discuss changes in a sales tracking system? The sales manager wants "minor" changes in the system, and the project leader in information technology is arguing that the changes are not minor.

Also, people cannot learn to negotiate in a controlled environment such as a workshop and expect to practice the strategies in real business situations. Everything is a variable in business, and the most significant variable is human emotions hidden under the cloak of expected corporate behavior. The only thing a person can control is his or her approach to negotiation.

Frequently, people raise this objection: "Negotiating with someone who shares your interest in the outcome is a lot easier than negotiating with someone who does not." The answer to this objection is contained in the process to come to a common goal, one of the Seven Rules that remove barriers that occur in negotiations.

SCHADENFREUDE

Does a person feel good when someone else loses? Does anyone feel good when the other person's head is hanging low from the shame of losing? In the business world, the more you make the person feel like a loser, the greater the chance of you becoming a loser in the long run—you win the toss but lose the relationship.

Mark's experience with his two managers illustrates the impact of making the other person feel like a loser. Mark led a marketing department where two senior managers, Emily and Rachel, reported to him. Each supervised a team of professionals. One day, Mark got three instant text messages on his cell phone from Emily, seeking an urgent meeting. When he called her, he sensed her frustration over the phone. She sounded distracted. She needed data from Rachel to complete an executive project by the end of that day. If

Emily submitted the project on time, she and her unit would receive recognition and additional funding for the project, and Mark's entire department would gain good visibility in the organization.

A real dilemma—how can Mark handle this situation without appearing to take sides or getting buried in the details? He took the plunge and called Rachel. She didn't wait for Mark to speak. Out came her angry outburst. After asking some probing questions, he gathered that Emily had circumvented the process for data requests and had copied Mark and a senior executive on her email request. It was a case of a hurt ego. It took time to shift Rachel's mindset and resolve the issue. To do this, Mark had to prove to Rachel that if they did not complete the project on time, the entire team, including Emily and Rachel, would suffer from the loss. If Emily did not meet the deadline, the whole department stood to lose; it was not a win-lose situation. "Emily's loss is not your gain, since we are on this road for the long haul."

Emily then sent Rachel a very conciliatory request for data. Rachel shifted her priorities. The agreement: Emily would not circumvent the process. She also promised to mention Rachel's contribution to her presentation. Emily completed the project on time! This agreement paved the way for good relations between Emily and Rachel, and recognition for Mark's department.

Every task could be a call for negotiation. Tara's story describing a weekly occurrence in her job is a perfect example of how every task at work could be a potential call for negotiation. Tara was an account specialist in a company that managed a sales system for large companies. The projects she worked on required a great deal of coordination among the support teams in her own company, but none of them reported to Tara. On a Friday afternoon, Tara got a call from a manager working for a corporate client, rushing through some changes he needed in the sales system within a week. The client manager kept repeating, "It is a top priority."

Tara was thinking, "I have to get back to the client. But before that, I need to check with my internal support resources that typically handle multiple projects from several clients. I am constantly fighting for these resources." Tara depended on many back-end resources—designers, coders, data analysts, and several other colleagues in her company's information technology department. The real negotiation she faced was not with the client but with her company's internal resources. Every time her client added a requirement, Tara had this massive task of negotiating with each of the support teams. She had to gain consensus from each group to get an estimate of time reasonable enough to accommodate the client. The individual resources had to take some time out from other client projects and get work done for her client.

Companies label this task as coordination or collaboration—all in the name of project management. You cannot always resort to escalation to higher-ups for resolution. This task is an all-out negotiation. When she gets estimates from internal resources, she breathes a sigh of relief. Not for too long, though, the fun part of negotiating with the client is yet to come. So, every step of the way, Tara has to gain consensus. Tara's problem might be familiar to every working person. Most likely, everyone negotiates daily with folks within the company. The following situations are common occurrences when someone works with clients:

- *Proposal and solution*—A client seeks options or proposals that can help them cut costs in a project you are overseeing.

- *Conflict and concern*—You did not meet deadlines, and the client is angry. But you know the reason for your delay: it was your client's ever-shifting priorities. How about a situation where the scope of the project has expanded? The original proposal was to create fifty reports; now the client wants an additional twenty-five, with new parameters. Although the scope has expanded, your client maintains that it has not changed.

- A *difference of opinion*—You are proposing changes to improve efficiency in a major client project. Suggestions from your colleague contradict your changes.

These are typical client scenarios. People probably encounter similar situations in other interactions at work with staff, managers, peers, vendors, business partners, and key stakeholders.

WHY IS NEGOTIATION SO DREADED?

Despite the many books and classes on negotiation, and experiences at work, people continue to suffer from misgivings when they hear the word "negotiation." The following comments express people's misgivings and fears about negotiating.

I avoid conflicts because I feel uncomfortable. My back-office support team doesn't agree with me about client deadlines. I see the loudest people winning in negotiations.

Clients are demanding. They change requirements and expect us to complete a project as scheduled within the set budget and timeframe. How can I say no to my clients? I don't want to lose the client. How can I negotiate without being confrontational? How do I collaborate with clients when we don't see eye-to-eye on what they want?

When clients change requirements, my boss wants me to ask for more resources from the client. I am caught between the client and my boss. Who said negotiations are win-win situations? Someone always loses. I feel like a loser even if I get my way, because I may have upset the client.

These comments show a clouding effect loaded with fear of results, *"us vs. them"* sentiments, distrust in the "other" people, and doubts about the negotiation process.

DO YOU TAKE ORDERS OR PROVIDE SOLUTIONS?

Everyone at work has heard the word *client*. Negotiations with *corporate clients* rank high on the scale of tough challenges. The meaning given in *Merriam-Webster* is: a client is "one that is under the protection of another." What you do should protect and benefit the client. This definition sets the stage for a good approach to negotiating with clients. Whatever you do should help you, too. A client with unreasonable daily demands weakens a consultant who is compliant, making it impossible to sustain a healthy, long-term relationship.

There is a distinction between external and internal clients. Some employees work directly with clients of the company, and others work with internal clients. Who are internal clients? They are the ones who fund projects in the company. If an employee is in market research, the sales division could be the employee's internal client. The sales division decides the budget for research and dictates the research they need. Most of the examples in this book address external clients, since these relationships are more challenging but vital to the company's profit. However, employees often have to negotiate with internal clients for budgets, resources, deadlines, changing priorities, and scope of projects.

. . . .

POWERFUL LEARNING

My training is titled *Soft, Yet Powerful Negotiations: Soft Approach, Powerful Impact.* The approach is soft because the class is not expected to adopt rigid rules prescribed by a textbook on negotiation. The word "powerful" does not mean learning how to do hard-core sales or labor negotiations to come out as winners. It is powerful when the focus is on long-term relationships, and both parties in a negotiation feel protected and empowered to make decisions.

. . . .

A business relationship cannot be one-sided. There must be a balance. You cannot always concede or compromise, or yield to a client's many wild requests, which exhausts available resources. You have to remain strong to protect the client. Continually nodding a yes to the client weakens your position. How can you protect someone when your position is weak? If you are weak, the client cannot lean on you.

Many professionals who are new to their jobs are not sure how to work with their corporate clients. They are juggling demanding clients, aggressive deadlines, reluctant internal back-end support teams, and profit-driven management. They struggle to find the balance between pleasing the client and doing what is right for the client. When the client says, "jump," some of these professionals ask, "how high?" and jump. And if they are not compliant, they are resisting or compromising, or in the worst case, they avoid taking client calls. They can change the way they think about their clients and see the pain behind the clients' complaints, changes, and demands.

These questions may help create a better focus on how to perceive client demands.

- Do I think about the pain that drives client behaviors?
- Have I taken the time to analyze my client's new requirements?
- Do these new requirements align with the client's business goals?
- Do these new demands solve a business problem?
- Do I share my concerns with the client when I know their demands are not beneficial to their business?

These questions will also trigger a change in your mindset. "Why don't we look at situations from the angle of what is beneficial to our clients? Why are we focusing on our pain or fears?" You will provide solutions to clients and not simply take orders. Raising these questions should be the beginning phase of any negotiation with clients. If they're not, any discussion with a client has to go into the "one wins, and the other loses" bin.

THE FOUR Ps OF NEGOTIATION

The key to success in negotiations is the shift in mindset from immediate gains to long-term relationships and business results. It sets the framework for using the right strategies in negotiations. Strategies revolve around four principal factors (Four Ps) that influence the whole process of negotiation, from defining the business problem to reaching an agreement. The Four Ps are "problem, process, people, and parameter" (see Figure 2).

Briefly, the definition of the Four Ps:

- *Problem* relates to the situation that warrants negotiation.
- *Process* is a set of sequential steps that begins with defining the problem and concludes with agreeing.
- *People* includes everyone involved in the negotiation, either directly or indirectly, from start to finish.
- *Parameter* is the boundary that affects the decisions. The budget is an excellent example of a limiting parameter.

FIGURE 2. The Four Ps.

The effectiveness of any strategy is a function of the Four Ps of negotiations. Most training programs concentrate on strategies to win. A sample list of topics covered in a typical training course on negotiation strategies include:

- Defining the business problem
- Best alternatives to solve the business problem
- "What if" scenarios to predict outcomes of alternatives
- Trade-offs—concessions you will make
- Conflict resolution. Dealing with difficult people— handling objections

- Mediation—competition, collaboration, and compliance in settling conflicts
- Strategies for in-person, telephone and, written venues for negotiation

These strategies are outward-focused, giving tips on how to handle the other person in the negotiation so that the outcome is a win, or a win-win for both. The contemplative mindset is inward-focused, asking the question, "What is my role in understanding the problem and bringing about a resolution?" The Four Ps organizes your thinking and helps you with a systematic approach. However, it requires a change in your *mindset* to engage the Four Ps within the framework of long-term relationships, and to maintain a balance between pleasing the client and doing what is right for the client and yourself.

Politeness and being productive are two additional attributes that come into play along with the Four Ps in influencing negotiation strategies (see Figure 3).

Being polite or courteous paves the way for smooth discussions. It keeps the topic on track and minimizes distractions. And there is no alternative to productivity, which means producing results. No matter how good your business relations are with the client, until you show productivity, no business relationship will be sustainable. Your performance, an outcome of your productivity, gives you credibility and offers leverage to present your options with confidence—we have done it, you know it, and you can trust us.

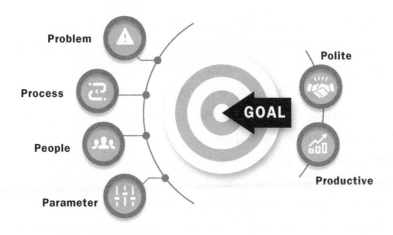

Problem

Process

People

Parameter

Polite

GOAL

Productive

FIGURE 3. Two More Ps.

Using the strategies without a shift in thinking is the reason so many people feel disillusioned about negotiation. Cindy managed a large project for a client. She maintained good relations with the client. The client frequently expanded the scope of her project, and she had to negotiate the cost and due dates for deliverables. Her boss sent her to training on negotiations where she learned some dealmaking strategies to win. Her biggest takeaway from the class was the approach to trade-offs. She went into client negotiations prepared with what she would give up and what she expected in return from the client. Her approach led to conflicts.

In every negotiation after the training, Cindy was prepared to give the client the extra marketing reports they demanded but expected them to extend the deadlines for delivering the reports. Her shortsighted focus on striking the trade-off left the clients unhappy and disrupted the relationship. Cindy's mind shift came when she realized that the trade-off should be between short-term wins and long-term business relationships, and not between reports and deadlines.

The eight principles for the right mindset, including The Communications Signal and the Seven Rules, yield results while maintaining business relationships. The many examples in the book will show the simplicity and directness of these principles. Whether you live in North America or in Europe, work in small business or large corporate, these principles work. How powerful would it be if everyone had a common understanding of these principles, and practiced them so that everyone would come together on a level playing field? It would give real meaning to the often used (or shall we say, misused) term "collaboration."

CHAPTER TWO

AVOID POTHOLES

The single biggest problem in communication
is the illusion that it has taken place.

—George Bernard Shaw

People often ask themselves, "Can we use the same tools and techniques for all our negotiations?" The more relevant question is, "Can we use the same approach regardless of the person with whom we are negotiating?" Most teachings on tools, techniques, and tips overlook differences in people. Work experience and cultural backgrounds are critical factors that influence one's approach to negotiation. If people try to negotiate in a style that does not fit them, or they are unaware of essential differences in the culture they are negotiating with, their negotiations can hit potholes. Culture can impede or slow down the negotiation process.

ONE STYLE DOES NOT FIT ALL

It is vital to define negotiation again: it is a relationship-driven process to reach an agreement with another person or entity to address a business opportunity or resolve a situation that is causing problems for both sides. The recap is a reminder that negotiation is an interactive process where people matter, and what influences them matters. A person's work environment exerts a critical influence on his or her negotiation style.

ENTREPRENEUR OR BIG CORPORATE?

After working for many years for major multinationals in corporate America, I ventured out as an independent consultant. Things were not as smooth as expected. Negotiation terms and my approach to clients lacked the independent-consultant style and resembled those of a manager in a big company. Two primary distinctions between the self-employed persons and the corporate employees come from the availability of resources to support their work and their dependence on others in decision-making.

In big corporate, you involve others in decision-making, because you depend on them to complete your work. If you work in marketing, you depend on several departments to launch an advertising campaign for a new product. You cannot pick a date for launching the campaign unless you receive the green light from other departments. You need product development to inform you when the product launch is scheduled, manufacturing to give an assurance that the product will be completed by the launch date, customer service to answer customer inquiries, sales to accept new orders, legal to approve the content for an advertising campaign, and agreement from the many business partners and vendors involved in the product launch.

When I switched to the self-employed status, I continued thinking "big corporate," still sitting in the driver's seat in control of corporate resources. I made commitments to clients that would require the support of an entire back office. A corporate client called me to deliver several talks on cross-cultural communications around the US within a thirty-day period. I was excited and agreed to the client's terms and conditions without checking my bandwidth to accommodate a major request that would typically require two speakers and a support team of three people.

The client project would require scheduling the talks, making travel arrangements, preparing the presentations and handout materials, holding discussions with client contacts, conducting assessments and getting feedback, and giving the talks, among other tasks. As an entrepreneur, to meet these commitments meant long hours and enormous resources. I did not have both. Unable to meet project deadlines, I lost the trust of a client, who then did not call me for the next consulting project. After this experience, I acknowledged that I did not have the resources I enjoyed in my corporate jobs and became more structured and realistic about my bandwidth for client projects.

After a five-year respite from corporate America, I went back. To my wonder, the same issues surfaced. Colleagues complained to me, "Try to remember that you are not an independent consultant anymore. You need to involve others in your decisions. You cannot function without their support and needed resources."

Entrepreneurs make their own decisions, and they do not have to get the corporate resources to draw on when they submit a proposal to clients. As an entrepreneur or small business owner, you have the freedom to decide, but financial considerations curtail your independence.

THE CULTURAL GAPS

Knowing differences in communication styles across countries is a must in negotiations. Cultural awareness is not an option; it is not one of the eight principles in this book; it is a necessity. Culture plays a predominant role in business communications and negotiations. Businesses operate across different international borders and cultural differences surface as barriers. Respecting differences paves the way for building long-term relationships.

This book is not dedicated to an in-depth discussion of the impact of various cultural differences on negotiations. By drawing a few comparisons between two countries with wide cultural gaps, such as the US and India, the book intends to sensitize you to the differences you may encounter in negotiations with people from other countries.

The three principles of cultural awareness are:

1. Know your own culture and the core values that drive your behavior before you learn about the other person's culture and core values.
2. Identify the core values where the widest gaps occur between both cultures. Bridge the gaps.
3. Don't judge people's behaviors without understanding their culture. Judging behaviors widens the cultural gaps, and acceptance closes it.

I have been giving talks since 2006 on cross-cultural communications between India and the US. In one talk, Steve, a vice president of operations, shared his experience, "I now realize that I made a mistake in evaluating one of my contract employees from India. He was an expert in his field, but he never spoke up in meetings. So, I assumed he did not know the answers. Your talk makes me realize why he remained silent when his manager or I was in the room. The reason is his cultural background in a hierarchical society. He was afraid to say something that would offend me, challenge the authority of his manager, or make the manager lose face in public. He would have broken the silence if his manager or I instructed him to speak up. If he knew that his silence bothered me, he would have shared his thoughts. The junior staff in my team tried to convince me that the contract employee shared his opinions freely with them." Making assumptions based on behaviors unfamiliar to you results in incorrect conclusions and decisions.

GO BEYOND BEHAVIORS TO IDENTIFY CORE VALUES

Awareness increases your ability to leverage a culture's strength. It is not about stereotypes where you expect people from one country to behave in a certain way. Country experts sometimes give out the top ten tips on handling people from another culture. When negotiators rely on tips given out by experts, they risk adjusting their behaviors to the other culture, without understanding the deep-seated values.

It is essential to look behind the practices to the core values of the culture. Each country has a set of core values. Respecting these values keeps harmony in business relationships. You cannot negotiate if you disrupt this harmony. A core value in the US is respect for one's independence. Companies encourage employees to express their opinions in meetings. Each employee expects a reward for individual contribution. It would break the harmony if management demanded silence from employees or did not recognize an individual's performance. The contrast to this is India's core value of a group mindset, where people shy away from the individual expression of ideas or recognition in meetings. Training programs or books on corporate negotiations often overlook cultural considerations. If the cultural values that drive your words and actions are unfamiliar to the others involved in the negotiation, you cannot have a shared understanding of the business problem and the options available to solve the problem. Misconceptions would govern these discussions.

CULTURAL DIFFERENCES AND THREE CORE VALUES

The three core values that most impact business communications between the US and India are *relationships, status,* and *time.* The three values combine to give rise to the contrast between a process-driven society and a people-driven society.

In the US, formal structure and processes make people more self-reliant and independent. A people-driven society like India relies on people to get work done. As a stranger, you can find your way in the US—not so in India. Even the residential addresses in India are not in sequential order. You are on G-Street and you are looking for door number 91. You breathe a sigh of relief because you reached door number 90 on G-Street. But, door number 91 is not next to door number 90, or even close to it. However, neighbors will walk you to door number 91 and perhaps also offer you a cup of coffee before taking you to your destination!

Relationships Matter

The main concepts underlying the relationship value in India are:

- Relationship-building precedes negotiations in India.
- People orientation means dependence on each other.
- Group or community mindset drives behaviors.
  "Saving face" is key.

Relationships directly impact negotiations. You can negotiate a business deal in the US with someone you don't know. It is a purpose-driven business relationship. In India and in most Asian countries, relationship-building precedes business discussions, if it is the first time both sides are engaging in a business transaction. It takes time. Group mindset, a product of the relationship factor, reigns in Asian countries. Who you know matters. What Tom experienced in India is an illustration of this cultural difference.

Tom went to India for the first time on a business trip to deliver training for a business client. He was excited. His first stop was Chennai, a major metropolitan city in the southern part of India. The client manager advised him to get handouts printed in Chennai, rather than printing and lugging them from the USA. Tom thought it was a good idea, and he engaged the services of a print shop in Chennai. Mohan, Tom's business colleague and friend in India, recommended a print shop owned by his distant cousin, Lata. Tom connected well with Mohan's cousin, Lata, who emailed Tom the final proofs and assured him that handouts would be ready the day he landed. Lata added that they could figure out delivery times after Tom landed in India. When Tom asked for specifics, Lata replied in her email, "Tom, don't worry. I will revert to you. Meet you at the hotel." Lata accepted Tom's credit card, and payment went through with no hiccups. Tom marveled at the technology that worked across borders.

Tom landed on a Friday, which turned out to be a major holiday, which meant all shops remained closed for three days. He had a two-day window before his flight to the training location. Tom was livid and called his colleague Mohan and ranted, "Why didn't Lata tell me? She promised me, and she didn't warn me about the holidays. Why didn't she drop off the materials at my hotel or hand them to you? I thought *revert* meant she would hand in the materials when she came to the hotel to meet me."

Tom spent the better part of the two days tracking Lata down. He called his client and explained the problem. Tom's client took this in stride and said, "Don't worry, Tom. It is a major holiday, and most small businesses remain closed. Why don't you email me a soft copy and we will make copies here? Then, go sightseeing."

Tom could not relax. Mohan tracked Lata down, and Lata left her grand family celebration to open the print shop and hand over the materials to Tom. She also brought him some mouth-watering goodies and invited him to her family celebration, which made Tom feel nostalgic for the many Indian parties he attended in the US and the variety of foods! How could he be mad at Lata?

He thanked her and learned two valuable lessons in culture. In India, people depend on each other to get things done. They neither have the process nor the inclination to be self-reliant. The second lesson pertained to the subtle differences between Indian and American English in emails. He later understood that revert meant that Lata would get back to him about the details, not that she would bring the handouts to the hotel. Tom was amazed that Mohan convinced Lata to leave a family celebration to open a print shop, and how Lata charmed him with the goodies. Leveraging relationships in negotiation averts mishaps.

In the US, printers give written confirmation of the pickup or delivery date along with timing and location. They leave nothing to chance. There is no question of tracking the owner when her shop closes for the holidays. It is not a personal relationship.

Here is another business example of the difference between process and people orientation. I traveled to many cities in the US to deliver my talks on multicultural communications. My client contacts raised in the US (for want of a better classification, I shall call them US Americans) asked for the date, time, agenda, and all the logistics about my training. Two weeks before my arrival, they emailed me their address along with a list of hotels and restaurants in the vicinity. My contacts arranged for me to get an ID badge to enter the building and a shuttle to pick up and drop me off at the hotel. They also provided two emergency contacts. Precision and process-orientation are two phrases that come to mind.

My non-US American client contacts (professionals who were in the US less than a year and had moved from India to the US to work at a client site) gave me the independence to figure it all out. Excitement or anxiety of uncertainty spiced up the experience every time I planned an out-of-state training program. However, they surprised me by showing up at the airport to pick me up or take me to an Indian restaurant, getting to know me—people orientation. In both cases, the training happened as scheduled. It is just the level of uncertainty that may drive one to distraction when working with the Indian point of contact. It depends on what people prefer. The certainty of process or the uncertainty laced with the warmth of the relationship.

Being a group mindset culture, Indians don't take that well to individual recognition in team meetings. Rather than enjoying the recognition, the individual would look upon it as other members of the team "losing face." It is not a *to each his own* culture. When a task is assigned to one person, others, even if they are not part of the team, will help to complete the work. It may not be visible to the outsider.

The close-knit group mindset has its drawbacks. It makes Indians a *compare and contrast* culture. Donna, a US American client, was not sure how to handle the salary negotiation with her staff member who had recently come to the US from India. The staff member was a technical genius and indispensable to her unit. He came to her and complained, "Every one of my friends is a manager with a salary exceeding mine, and along with a 20 percent bonus, the take-home pay is twice my total compensation. I am the only one with the title of technical analyst. I am losing face in my community."

In the US, with an independent mindset, people don't discuss titles and compensation in social gatherings or with anyone, even at work. Donna explained to her staff member, "I understand your situation, but it is not practical for managers to consider social pressure when deciding to give promotions or salary increases. Promotions are based on individual performance, and I will be glad to consider you for a promotion when the new project is completed. You are an extremely capable person and a valuable member of my unit." Donna carefully avoided using such comparative phrases, as, "*Unlike your country, we in the US* don't promote people based on social pressure." Comparisons widen cultural gaps. The staff member accepted her explanation.

Respect for Status

Relationship and status are related topics. The underlying concepts of status are:

- Silence is not a strategy, but a mark of respect for authority.

- Job titles matter in negotiations.
- Direct and indirect styles of speaking create conflicts.

Jane was in charge of the automated sales support system for the company. She was a vice president of the division. She was adding new features to the system and chose a vendor based in India. The vendor's employees worked onsite at client locations in the US. She convened a virtual meeting to discuss some problems that surfaced when implementing the new features in the system. She was not happy with the new deadlines set by the vendor. Karan, the director of the vendor team, and the product experts from his vendor team spread across several locations in the US, attended the virtual meeting. Jane opened the meeting expressing her concerns about delays and demanded that they complete the project on time. She wanted to know the reason for the delay.

The vendor's product experts knew that some members of Jane's team caused the delays because they were continually changing requirements. Jane asked the experts directly if they knew the reason. There was dead silence. If you were in Jane's shoes, you would walk away, concluding that the experts' silence was an admission of guilt. Karan, the vendor's director intervened, apologized, and agreed to meet the deadlines set by Jane. This silence of the Indian experts, who did not speak up in front of their boss or their client, caused incorrect conclusions and decisions. When Jane found out the truth from the vendor's director, she was livid. She gave a piece of her mind to her staff about honesty and to the experts in the vendor's team about their silence. If you are a client from the US, you are likely to misconstrue the other person's silence as an acceptance or as a strategy to unnerve you or as a sign that he or she did not know the answer.

Most people from India will maintain a polite silence in meetings even if they disagree with what their clients or managers are saying. Respect given by the subordinates varies with their education levels, work experience, exposure to western influence, and residency in a rural city or a big city like Mumbai.

Here's an example on the personal front. It was in the 1990s, and an Indian colleague signed up for a weight-loss program. She had been in the US for less than a year. During the whole class, the weight scale was the only piece that made sense to her. There was nothing on the food list for an Indian vegetarian. Being Indian, she asked no questions, out of respect for the instructor. Her weight remained the same and so did her eating habits. The only thing she lost was money—the program fee.

Indians either give-in—concede, compromise—or avoid if they have to negotiate with people in authority. Negotiations in India happen behind closed doors with people of equal status or job titles, perhaps to avoid confrontations in the presence of junior staff. Meetings may end up being a venue to announce the decisions.

Sometimes as simple a matter as seating arrangement can affect negotiations. Let's say you were presenting a proposal to Asians and the negotiation failed. You may walk away with the wrong conclusion that the terms were simply unacceptable. It may be inconceivable to you that a cultural mix-up could be at the bottom of this failure; however, you did not give the Asian executive the seat at the head of the table. And to add insult to injury, you were addressing your comments to a manager in the executive's staff, and not the executive himself. You went further and called the executive by his first name, even though you are not equal in status to him.

Most US Americans in a business setting are relatively direct in conveying a message. They get to the point. Indians are politely indirect and get around to the point. How would you interpret the following conversation between Harry, a client in the US and Ravi, a member of the vendor team in India?

Harry says, "Ravi, we need to discuss the project. My director is not happy with the progress and wants an update first thing Monday morning. I have scheduled an early morning conference call tomorrow (Saturday, India time[1]), and three of us will call in from New York. I want you and two of your team leads to attend. Send me the names of the two leads."

Ravi: "Yes, yes."

---

1 India is about ten hours ahead of New York. So, an early Saturday morning India time is Friday night in New York.

· 3 5 ·

Harry: "Good. That's settled."

Ravi: "My sister is getting married this Sunday near Palamaneri. I invited my team to the wedding."

Harry: "Enjoy the wedding."

On Friday night, New York time, Harry was ready with his
team members to carry on with the discussions. To his
embarrassment, no one from the Indian team turned up for
the conference call. Ravi did not respond to his desperate
calls or texts. Because of this event, Harry had doubts about
Indian work ethics and commitment, and he concluded: "I
cannot trust these guys anymore."

The Indian side—everyone in India knows that weddings
are all-day affairs, sometimes lasting over three days. So, if the
marriage was on Sunday, pre-wedding events started Friday
night India time. Indian tradition mandates attendance of
all family members. Weddings are fun and noisy events, and
phone connections are bad if they happen in a rural area.
Ravi had indicated he would not come and that he would be
near Palamaneri, which is probably a rural area with limited
phone connections, and perhaps, his entire work team would
be at the wedding party.

Harry was not familiar with India's geography, let alone
names of villages, or the Indian's polite and indirect style of
conveying a message. How would he know about wedding

customs in India? He had never visited India, nor had he been a guest at an Indian wedding. Ravi spoke fluent English, and Harry asked no questions, so the thought of cultural differences never crossed their minds. Indirect style of conversation manifests in the Indian's daily negotiation with clients, management, and suppliers. Ravi's indirect "no" was not audible to Tom's US American "tell it like it is" ears.

US Americans and people in India have different ways of expressing themselves that often lead to many misunderstandings. Here is another example of indirect speech:

> The US American asks, "Can you send me the report this Friday?"
> The Indian says, "Yes, yes, I'll try."
> The US American says, "Good."

Privately, the US American thinks, "Okay, she sounds enthusiastic, and she will most likely do it." The Indian thinks, "What a relief; he understands that I cannot do it." *I'll try* is a polite way of saying no in India. And, "yes, yes" means she heard him, it does not mean that she agreed with the US American.

People in the US respect authority, but they respect the work process and outcomes more. It saves time when you are direct. So, when Indians are politely indirect in their response, the "no" escapes the notice of the US worker. Indians' indirect style of conveying a message is in contrast to the more direct style of US Americans. In the US, it is misleading to say, "I'll try" when it is a "no" to project requests. In India, it is rude to say no. The direct style of speaking clashes with the indirect to cause havoc in negotiations, unless both parties understand and acknowledge cultural differences.

What holds Indians back from saying an outright "no," pushing back, or asking for more time? A phenomenon I knew growing up in India—*status*, or respect for authority. It is insulting to challenge a client or boss. Even if client demands are unreasonable and their statements are inaccurate, Indians "save face" of people in authority by being silent or politely indirect. It is especially true of people from less urban areas, where old Indian traditions linger.

Time Is Not Money

The underlying concepts:

- There is no compensation for delays.
- Work styles differ.
- "*Kaal*" is passage of time.

Rekha invited her colleague, Susan, to a classical Indian music concert. The concert was scheduled to start at 5:00 p.m. with dinner to follow at 7:00 p.m. Susan asked her if it would be a formal event. Rekha replied, "Yes, Susan, you can come a little early to get parking." Susan came a half-hour early to get parking. She was dressed in her formal black gown. When Susan arrived, the parking lot was empty and Rekha was nowhere to be seen. She parked her car and went into the reception area to check if she was in the right place. The huge poster of the concert confirmed that she was in the right place.

Around 5:30 p.m., people started coming. The women were dressed in colorful Indian outfits. Rekha came in around 6:00 p.m. and greeted Susan with a broad smile. Susan asked her, "You told me to come early, and you didn't tell me not to wear black."

Rekha replied in a gentle tone, "Susan, Indians rarely wear black and we are early. The musicians' flight is late. They are not coming until 7:00 p.m. So, we will have dinner before the concert."

Susan tried to hide her frustration and said, "Does everyone know about this delay? Is that why they are coming in late?"

Rekha casually replied, "Late? No, we don't expect these concerts to start at the scheduled time. So, we come in when it is convenient for us."

Susan thought, "If it were an opera, I would have walked out or demanded a refund. How do the Indians take the delay in stride without getting agitated? Why was there no announcement about the delay?" The point here is not that Indians are always late. They are not. Most concerts start and conclude on time. Most business meetings start and conclude on time. What surprises the US Americans is that Indians accept delays without looking for compensation for lost time.

Each culture has a different working style, and if you don't recognize the differences between cultures, many problems can surface. The US American is time-conscious and structured in thinking. Goals, strategies, a uniform process to get the work done, expectations including due dates, progress updates, and alerts or heads-up about delays, and the infamous dashboard of such company performance measures as sales revenue, profit margin, customer retention, and cash flow, are features of the US corporate world. When business tasks are assigned to US Americans, they will ask such questions as, "When do you want this done? What about my other projects? What is the order of priority?" In the US, timeliness and accuracy are critical measures of an individual's performance at work.

Indians multitask and are not likely to ask time-driven questions. Companies in the US outsource work to India for cost reasons and for technical know-how. Being a people-driven hierarchical society, Indians will accept multiple tasks expecting they can do it in due time with the help of people in their network. And, it is not in their culture to say no to clients or anyone in authority. When you assign a task to an Indian, he or she will not push back and ask, "When is it due? Do you want me to set aside other priorities? I don't understand the task, can you please explain?" The thought of negotiating does not even enter the multitasking unstructured mind. The Indian's willingness to take on tasks without questioning is gratifying to the US American until it is time for completion of the assigned tasks. Then comes the cultural shock.

Standardization is another component of the time value of money where the gap is wide between the US and India. The basic purpose of standardization in business is to enforce consistency and uniformity in processes within the company, so the work gets done efficiently. Most of the schools in India don't ask the students to show the steps they used to solve a problem in math, and they do not encourage students to ask questions. This practice carries through in the Indian's style of work. Indians solve technical problems with great ease, but the process to solve the problem may not be repeatable or measurable, which are two components of standardization. And, many Indians are not accustomed to explaining how they got to the solution. What you cannot explain, repeat, or measure is unlikely to have consistency or uniformity. How do you work across cultures when the gap is so wide? If you are process-driven, and you have to work with companies in India, then take the time to standardize the work processes to meet your expectations, and train the Indian team on the processes. If the clients do not take the time upfront to standardize and train, they may lose the savings they expected from working with the technical experts in India. The time required for process training is an important consideration when you are negotiating with Indians.

Time is not money for a people-driven multitasking culture. The word *kaal* means time in India. *Kaal* is a fluid term signifying the passage of time, not the small hand and the big hand of a clock. In the US, time lost is money lost. In the earlier example of the US client, Harry lost valuable time because of Ravi's sister's "Indian wedding." From the Indian perspective, Ravi would have "lost his face" in his community if he did not engage in the wedding, and if he did not involve his staff in the festivities. The Indian's perspective of time differs from the US American's.

Such differences disrupt harmony when people from one culture engage in business with people from an unfamiliar culture. What is needed is an understanding of the core values of the other cultures they will encounter in their business interactions. It is an understanding that will enable people to accept different styles and leverage critical strengths in each culture to bring about a success in negotiations. It requires patience to learn.

Note: I base the differences between India and the US in this chapter on cultural behaviors to show what happens when one country interacts with another on business matters without understanding each other's cultures. The cultural behaviors of Indians should not be confused with the Eastern philosophy originating in ancient Indian teachings, which is the foundation for this book.

THE *CHAKRA* OF NEGOTIATION PRINCIPLES

This section lays out the eight principles of negotiation and sets the chakra, or wheel, in motion for learning the contemplative mindset, which is the essence of the ancient teachings of India. The Communications Signal in the upcoming chapter three is the first principle of negotiations, and describes the process to reach a shared understanding of the business problem. The Seven Rules are described in the remaining chapters.

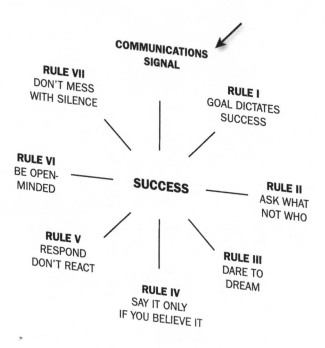

FIGURE 4. The *Chakra* of Negotiation Principles.

THE COMMUNICATIONS SIGNAL

If we can understand the problem, the
answer will come out of it, because the
answer is not separate from the problem.

—J. Krishnamurti

B efore you engage in any business interaction—meetings, presentations, or negotiations—it is best to understand the true meaning of communication (see Figure 5).

. . . .

TELL, CONVEY, AND COMMUNICATE

The three keywords, Tell, Convey, and Communicate, are not dictionary words. I am taking the liberty here of using them in a corporate sense—not in common sense—in the same way we distinguish between selling and marketing in the business world. Tell, Convey, and Communicate are levels of any business conversation. This graphic of the traffic signal characterizing the three levels of a conversation is used as a starting point in my training programs.

. . . .

COMMUNICATIONS AND THE TRAFFIC SIGNAL

I was at the traffic signal at a major intersection. The light just turned from yellow to red. I stopped and impatiently waited for green. Even after the green light was on, I looked in all directions to make sure I could move forward. Why? I had to be safe and make sure everyone was following the

TELL — REACT

CONVEY — RESPOND

COMMUNICATE — ACT

FIGURE 5. The Communications Signal

same rules—observing the traffic signal to reach a common understanding that it was safe to move forward. Sometimes people try to beat the red light, and crashes can occur. This traffic signal characterizes the three levels of a conversation: Tell, Convey, and Communicate. It is essential to understand this concept of communication before engaging in any negotiation.

What is the difference between communication and conversation? In my definition, *communication is a conversation that leads to a common understanding in any discussion.*

Conversations can be one-sided because people don't always listen with an open mind. Imagine a conversation between two colleagues, Todd and Sally, who are working together on a marketing brochure for a new product. Todd had decided to go with a new vendor to produce the brochure. Sally had no preference, and she is presenting her reasons for choosing an existing vendor based on his track record of accuracy, pricing, and timeliness. Todd is not listening to Sally because his mind is preoccupied with his reasons for choosing the new vendor. They will not reach a common understanding of the right choice of vendor for their project when one person is not listening with an open mind.

Communication means common understanding.

It is amusing to see email messages saying, "I communicated *to* Tina the content of our discussion. The ball is in her court."

No, the ball is still floating in midair!

"Communicate" and "to" cannot be used in the same sentence. You can "tell" or "convey" because those actions are one-sided. But you cannot communicate one-sidedly. There is no good or bad communication. There is only communication (or the lack of it), and it means reaching a common understanding.

Communication, by its very sound, implies an interactive exchange to reach a common understanding. Going back to the situation between Todd and Susan, a conversation took place, but the two people did not walk away with a shared understanding. Each position on the traffic signal is like each level of a conversation.

FOLLOW THE SIGNAL TO COMMUNICATIONS

RED LIGHT: TELL–REACT

When you *tell* people something, it is like a red light—people will only *react*. The conversation is one-sided. You can tell an audience that the customer satisfaction score is just 30 percent. It is data with no background, message, or insights. The listeners stop. They can only react to this piece of information. They will be surprised, upset, angry, indifferent, accusatory, or quiet. These are all reactions. What is a "reaction?" It is a surface-level, immediate, sometimes emotional way of addressing any situation. There is no pause before action.

There is no better illustration of a tell–react situation than a parent-teenager conversation.

The Authoritarian Dad

Most of you are familiar with typical conversations between parents and their teenage children. There is no better illustration of "telling." It is mostly one-sided. Take the example of Matt, a teenager, and his dad.

Father says, "Matt, you cannot stay out after 9:00 p.m."

Matt reacts, "That's not fair, Dad."

Father says, "Sorry, be back before 9:00 p.m. That is my rule."

It stops Matt from engaging in any further conversation. Matt's reaction: anger, storming out of the room or, even worse, sneaking out at night.

When you tell people something without opening up the opportunity for a dialogue, you can only expect them to react.

The Unfair Boss

Conversations in business meetings are no better. Most are full of bright red lights. Here is a manager's conversation with a junior analyst:

She tells the analyst in her staff, "You are not getting a salary increase or bonus this year."

The analyst reacts, "Oh! That is not fair. I worked hard for it. How come Penny got a promotion last month?"

Manager's Way or the Highway

Think of the many team meetings where the project manager puts up a slide and tells the team, "For the next three months, our team will work on this top-priority project. Here is the approach I want you to take."

The team can only react to this statement. If the boss's approach is unpopular with the team, how does the team react? Compliance, open resistance, passive resistance, complaints, and sabotage are common reactions.

People take a stand when you tell them something.

They think:

- I like it.
- I don't like it—I'm angry.
- It's personal—manager dislikes me!
- I don't care.
- It is not rational—there is no reason for cuts!

Depending on the stand they take, people accept, disapprove, or say nothing. Some show anger or vent to colleagues, while others dust off their résumés.

So, when you tell, you open yourself up to unlimited interpretations. In negotiations, when you tell your options, the other person takes a stand. "Telling" and "taking a stand" have a cause-and-effect connection.

YELLOW LIGHT: CONVEY–RESPOND

The next level of conversation is conveying a message, which makes the listener pause, think, let it absorb, and then respond.

The Authoritarian Dad

Let us redesign the parent-teenager conversation, where the parent gives a message behind his command:

> Matt, I am fine with you going to the party. But I am concerned for your safety. You know about recent crimes. It is best you return by 9:00 p.m.

The message here is the parent's concern for his son's safety. It gives a reason he told his son to return by 9:00 p.m. So, what does the son do with this message? He pauses, thinks about it, and sees how he can respond to it. That is why this message is similar to the yellow light—it helps people pause before responding.

The Unfair Boss

The manager gives a message along with the announcement of salary cuts in a staff meeting: "Our company has lost a huge account. Income has dropped significantly. We froze salaries and cut out bonuses. I see it as a temporary situation. No one will get any increases or bonuses for this year unless things turn around."

Her staff analysts pause to think: The company is facing financial problems. But they care, so rather than laying people off, they opted to freeze salaries. How does this impact me? What about my vacation plans? Do I need to look for another job?

Manager's Way or the Highway

Imagine if a manager presents his/her approach for the project to a team this way:

We are on a tight budget. So, I propose this approach for our project. I have tried it before. It is efficient, has a short learning curve, and is less taxing on the team.

Team members pause to think: What does this mean for me? How will it impact me?

This conversation is still one-sided, but it adds information and ideas to influence thinking. The message provides background on the company's tight budget and the manager's interest in the team's learning curve and effort. The listeners are not reacting or taking a stand.

GREEN LIGHT: COMMUNICATE–ACT

Communication in business is a journey to reach a common understanding. This journey is similar to the *path to understanding* of Eastern philosophy. How does it happen? What are the steps along the way? There are five sequential steps to set the stage for negotiation (see Figure 6).

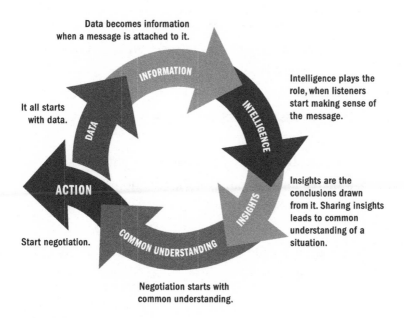

FIGURE 6. The Journey from Data to Common Understanding

- *Data*—It all starts with data.
- *Message*—Data becomes information when a message is attached to it.
- *Intelligence*—When the listener thinks about the message and tries to make sense of it, and validates the message, he gains intelligence.
- *Insights*—Insights are the conclusions drawn from intelligence. Insights answer three questions in solving business problems:
  1. *So What?*—So what does this message mean for me? How am I impacted?

2. *Why Care?*—Why should I care about it? What will I lose if I ignore the message? What will I gain if I take action to address the problem?

3. *What Next?*—What action steps should I take to address the problem? How soon should I take any action?

- *Common Understanding*—Sharing insights leads to a shared understanding of the situation. This is the green signal to go!

Negotiation should start with this shared or common understanding.

COMMUNICATION IS THE PROCESS OF TRANSFORMING DATA INTO INSIGHTS TO REACH A COMMON UNDERSTANDING

The data-to-insights journey is like the traffic signal. Here is a typical route of data to insights, and what happens if you start negotiations at each of the stages, from data to shared insights:

Red Light	Tell-*Stop*	Data ▸ ***React***/Take Stand ▸ *Bargain*
Yellow Light	Convey-***Pause***	Information ▸ ***Respond***/Analyze ▸ Intelligence ▸ *Inconclusive*
Green Light	Communicate-***Go***	Insights ▸ Open Dialogue ▸ Shared Insights ▸ Common Understanding ▸ ***Act*** ▸ *Negotiate*

Data is one-sided telling. It is a red light for you to *stop*. Most people react or take a stand when they hear data. At this stage, you can only bargain. Bargaining is a one-time event focusing on terms and conditions, without regard to long-term relationships and results. Bargainers tend to focus on one aspect such as pricing. Unfortunately, most so-called negotiations start at the data stage.

Information is conveying a message. It is a yellow light for you to *pause*. This is the time for you to think, analyze, and validate what you heard and make sense of it and gain intelligence. At the information stage, any attempt at negotiation would create confusion and inconclusive outcomes.

Insights are the conclusions from the intelligence. You see the green light. But you are discussing with others to reach a common understanding before you move forward. It is the same as looking around both ways to make sure everyone is observing the traffic rules before you move forward. Once you have reached a common understanding, you can start negotiations.

Here is a more in-depth look into the whole process of reaching a common understanding of any situation, with the example of the manager of a customer service call center and the results of a customer satisfaction study.

RED LIGHT: TELL–STOP–REACT

Data Stage. Data could be facts and figures that are not connected to give you a clear message. Here is a set of data points from the customer satisfaction study presented by a research analyst to the customer call center manager.

Customer satisfaction rating is 2.5 on a scale of 1 to 5, with 5 being the most satisfied. This rating is a significant drop from the prior year. Only 30 percent are happy with the support they received for the new product. Sixty percent of customers report dissatisfaction with the support they received from the call center agents. The complaints: "Agents never pick up the phone. There is a long hold time before they get to an agent. Each agent gives a different explanation for the product." Attrition or churn rate has increased to 10 percent in six months.

YELLOW LIGHT: CONVEY–PAUSE–RESPOND

Respond goes through information, intelligence, and insights stages.

Information Stage. The message from the satisfaction study is that customers are not happy with the support services for the new product and the company is losing customers rapidly.

Intelligence Stage. It is the analysis or *thinking and validation* stage when you try to make sense of the message, or validate it with other data or information. The key questions here are: "Do I have all the data? Am I missing key data? Do I trust the message? How can I confirm the message?" The call center manager gains the intelligence when he returns

THE COMMUNICATIONS SIGNAL

to his office after the presentation. He asks himself, "Are the customers unhappy with the product, the technical support, or the way the call center is handling inquiries? Are the sales teams misleading the customers about the benefits of the product?" He listens to a few customer calls, attends sales presentations, and talks to the senior level staff of his call center team.

Insights Stage. At this stage, the manager draws conclusions. The picture is getting clearer for him after he assembles the information from various sources. The ah-ha moment occurs when he zeros in on the problem and knows how to address the issue. The support service for the product was the problem, and the issue was the lack of consistent training for the support service agents in the new product. Many of the agents were giving out incorrect answers to customer inquiries and causing confusion and frustration among customers. The call center manager thought, "This is a quick fix. We can train the agents and educate the customers. But, I need to negotiate with management for the training and education budgets." For an experienced professional in analytical roles, one thing becomes crystal clear. *If you get to the right problem, the right solution is not far off.*

GREEN LIGHT: COMMUNICATE–GO–ACT

Common Understanding Stage. The call center manager does not go for negotiations immediately after he understands the problem and possible solutions. He is in the looking-around stage to make sure it is safe to go. He calls a meeting of those people involved in the new product, namely sales, product development, technical support, marketing, and senior members of his staff to share his insights. The discussions lead to a common understanding of the problem and potential solutions.

The green signal is given to move forward with the negotiation. Imagine what would happen if you ran a red light, tried to rush through before the yellow turned red, did not wait for the green light at a four-way intersection, or failed to look around to make sure no other car was ignoring the traffic signal? A crash? A collision? The same thing happens when you negotiate at the data or information stage. Most negotiations happen at the data stage, and then negotiators blame the people and process, or the techniques learned in books or training programs!

You cannot negotiate until you are at this stage of common understanding. Initially, it may take time to go from data to insights. However, with the repeated implementation of this process, it becomes a habit. If you react as soon as clients add new requirements, you can only bargain and barter at this point. You are at the data stage. The client is telling you what they want, and you are taking a stand.

The three scenarios, Authoritarian Dad, Unfair Boss, and Manager's Way, are revised to show the right way to reach a common understanding before negotiating.

Authoritarian Dad

The parent-teenager conversation is transformed into "communication." The dad opens the line of communication.

Father: "Matt, are you going to the party tonight?"

Matt: "Yes, Dad."

Father: "What time are you coming home?"

Matt: "My friends and I are planning to be back by midnight."

Father: "Are you going out with Greg and Steve?"

Matt: "Yes, and Roger is joining us, too. He is the new kid you met yesterday."

Father: "Who is driving?"

Matt: "Greg."

Father: "I'm glad you are going with your friends. However, I am concerned for your safety because of recent crimes and accidents after teenage parties. I emailed you the articles, remember? I think it's best you return by 9:00 p.m. I have an early morning meeting tomorrow, and you have a test."

Matt: "That's too early. The party is only just getting started at 9:00 p.m.; that's when it starts to get fun. I'll be a laughingstock if I leave that early, and Greg and Steve won't agree to it."

Father: "Okay, Matt. I care about your safety, and you don't want to be the odd man out. Let's figure something out."

Parent and teenager pause to think. Both come to an understanding that one is concerned about safety and the other about perception. Not that Dad is stubborn, and the kid is reckless. They now know each other's point of view. Both understand the limitations and think about options. Now begins the negotiation.

Unfair Boss
Salary Cuts—Low Budgets—Let's Talk!

Manager to staff: "Our company has lost a huge account and our financial figures reflect it. How many of you have seen it? What do you think? Senior management doesn't want layoffs and believes a salary freeze is our best alternative."

This kind of information-sharing will open the dialogue and get management and staff to come to a shared understanding of issues and actions. Instead of reaction, what you get is a more responsible action from everyone where they discuss the issue: "What can we do and how can each of us contribute to the solution?"

Manager's Way or the Highway

Now, the manager opens the dialog and discusses the approach for a project to the team this way:

"I am proposing this approach because we are on a tight budget. I have tried this before and it is efficient, has a short learning curve, and is less taxing on the team. I am open to your suggestions for a new approach or modifications to this approach. Any thoughts?"

Team members ask questions and give ideas and suggestions to change the approach. The manager and team now have a plan that will work because there is a buy-in from both sides.

IT'S ALL IN THE TIMING

A client-vendor example further illustrates the importance of timing in negotiation. Cathy's team is managing a CRM (customer relationship management) system for a client. Michael is the manager in the client's sales division. Michael is making new demands for additional sales reports.

RED LIGHT: TELL–STOP–REACT

Data Stage

Michael [*client*]: I need additional sales reports.

Cathy [*vendor*]: When?

Michael [*client*]: June 15.

Cathy [*vendor*]: That's the same date as other deliverables. Can you send me a quick email with specifications? I'll run it through my unit to get cost and time estimates. *Cathy does not react or take a stand, but she stops and asks for more data.*

YELLOW LIGHT: CONVEY–PAUSE–RESPOND

Information Stage

Michael: I'll email you the details; however, I must warn you we have no cushion in our budget. We need the reports on June 15th.

Cathy: Are these reports also for the sales division?

Michael: Yes. A senior executive has requested these reports. He needs them before the executive council meeting. *Michael gives Cathy a message that the request came from a senior executive.*

Intelligence Stage (Thinking and Validating)

Cathy pauses. She is making sense of Michael's request. She is thinking, "The client's budget is tight. I have proof that the new sales reports are for an executive council meeting. We have to do them. I can defer the older requests. I have room for negotiation. I am looking for new business opportunities from this client and they are looking for vendors to design new sales performance reports for senior executives. I want Michael to give my company the opportunity. This request from Michael may be a door opener for the bigger opportunity, since the executive council will get to see the sales reports. It gives my company the visibility we need for future projects."

Cathy receives an email from the client. She brainstorms with her team managers. The managers are concerned about the complexity of the sales reports and their workload, and estimate that their staff will have to work overtime—meaning evenings and weekend hours—if the client does not postpone other projects. They ask Cathy to either request payment from the client for overtime to do the additional reports or postpone the other projects. If Michael does not agree to pay, Cathy will have to figure out a way to cover overtime expenses with her budget. She calculates the potential income from new opportunities.

Insights Stage

Cathy comes to an understanding of the problem and the solution. She has to do the new sales reports requested by

Michael, even though the new request is complex and expensive. The client may not postpone other projects or pay for overtime. Cathy is interested in expanding the relationship to include executive dashboard reports, and the new request is a door opener. The expected income from the client for the dashboard reports may outweigh the cost of overtime for doing the new report requested by Michael.

GREEN LIGHT: COMMUNICATE–GO–ACT

Common Understanding Stage

Cathy requests a meeting with Michael to come to a shared understanding of the situation. Both Michael and Cathy understand the complexity and cost of doing the sales reports for the executive, and they also recognize the necessity of doing them. Both are keen on using the new reports as a prototype for other executives. The budget is tight for the client, and staff resource constraints challenge Cathy.

The planning for negotiation begins now!

There is a common thread among great negotiators: they follow the basic rules of communication. Violation of these rules causes disrupted business relationships. It is not about winning in a discussion or debate. It is about negotiating in such a way that everyone feels a sense of involvement and contribution.

Expanding your role in client organizations, enlisting the long-term support of your immediate and extended teams, and collaborating with your business partners are more critical than showing a few wins. Keeping a client is more meaningful than sticking to terms and conditions in every negotiation. This approach is the sign of a contemplative mindset.

The upcoming chapters explain the remaining principles of negotiation, The Seven Rules for success.

YOUR GUIDE TO THE COMMUNICATIONS SIGNAL

- Red—Tell–React
- Yellow—Convey–Respond
- Green—Communicate–Act

Communication is a conversation that concludes in common understanding.

STAGES OF COMMUNICATION

- Data–Information–Intelligence–Insights–Shared Insights–Common Understanding
- Wait for the green signal before negotiating.

What will happen if we negotiate at the data stage?

THE SEVEN RULES

The Seven Rules may not be unique or new to the business world. The foundation for these rules is in the ancient Indian teachings. The elements of each rule along with the examples, stories, and cases give a fresh and perhaps a practical way of applying the rules in negotiations. The case study titled "Adrift Website" appears in most chapters of the book to show how the elements roll into each of the Seven Rules. This Adrift Website Case is about a client who requests a vendor to build a new and improved website, after failed attempts by other website designers. It is a real case, but names have been changed. The Seven Rules are:

Rule I. Goal Dictates Success
Rule II. Ask What, Not Who
Rule III. Dare To Dream
Rule IV. Say It Only If You Believe It
Rule V. Respond, Don't React
Rule VI. Be Open-Minded
Rule VII. Don't Mess With Silence

CHAPTER FOUR

RULE I.
GOAL DICTATES SUCCESS

WHERE ARE WE?

S o far, you have read the difference between wins and
success in negotiation, the importance of the right
mindset, and the role of timing in negotiation, as well
as a warning not to start the negotiation at the data stage, but
to wait until the green signal for a common understanding of
the problem. The next phase is setting the goal for negotiation, which is Rule I in The *Chakra* of Negotiation Principles.
The *Goal Dictates Success* in a negotiation, so it has to be cho-
sen wisely (see Figure 7).

FIGURE 7. Rule I: The *Chakra* of Negotiation Principles.

ELEMENTS OF RULE I

- Set Clear Goals
- Reflect The Needs Of Both Sides
- Use *We*, Not *Us vs. Them*
- Focus On Needs

SET CLEAR GOALS

It is important to create a clear framework for setting a wise goal. The Opening Thoughts section explained intention, dream, and goal within the context of Eastern philosophy. Now, you will see the relevance of these concepts in setting a goal for negotiation. A goal is a realistic and measurable target established to guide the negotiation with the business relationship in mind. Intention and dream are essential for choosing and achieving a goal. Intention is a state of mind, which helps frame and manifest your goals.

For instance, you intend to build a long-term relationship with clients, and that drives your goals, behaviors, and business interactions. If you aim to outwit your client or competition, your goals, thoughts, words, and actions will mirror your intention. A dream paves the way for hope and sets the mood. Success is not possible if you approach negotiation with doom and gloom. It would be best if you had all three—dream, intention, and goal—to balance your business interactions.

Most entrepreneurs have to present their idea or product to investors. They give mock presentations before they take it to the potential investor. One entrepreneur defined his goal for the investor presentation as, "Get money from the investor." Building a relationship or making the investor wealthy did not appear to be the intention in this goal. His goal did not reflect his dream of sharing his innovative idea to benefit a large group of customers. The goal had a narrow, one-sided focus, and it set the tone for his mock presentation. The pitch lacked the passion with which he normally talked about his idea. The goal that might have generated audience interest in the entrepreneur's mock presentation: prove to investors that the market demand for his innovative idea exceeded expectations, and his intention was to generate a rapid return on investment.

Most negotiations miss the mark because the goal is not clear or is perhaps too narrow or short term in focus.

WHAT ARE UNCLEAR AND NARROWLY FOCUSED GOALS?

Two business scenarios show examples of unclear and narrow goals.

Business Scenario One

Proposal for cost cut. A vendor is working with a client on a marketing project. The client announces a 20 percent cut in the project and asks the vendor to submit a proposal for completing this project on time with no changes to the original project requirements. It upsets the vendor, and he reacts to this data by coming up with two alternative goals for negotiating with the client:

- Goal 1: Make up for the cost cut by making the client pay in other ways.
- Goal 2: Cut down my work by 20 percent to match the client's cost cut.

Goal 1 is a perfect example of an unclear goal. It is difficult to measure, since you don't know if you can quantify "making the client pay in other ways."

Goal 2 is a reaction with a narrow or short-term focus. The vendor is taking a stand based on customer demand.

After looking back at the relationship with the client, he comes up with Goal 3.

Goal 3 is to preserve the current quality of the project measured by zero defects and a four-week turnaround of deliverables.

The vendor who intends to maintain the relationship with the client and focus on long-term business outcomes would choose Goal 3. This goal reflects the intention of the vendor to be a partner, interested in the client's projects. The client would not want the vendor to cut costs at the expense of quality. With such a shared goal, the vendor and the client become partners in finding innovative ways to address the problem of budget cuts without sacrificing quality. The client now perceives this situation as "our" problem and not just the vendor's problem.

Business Scenario Two

Scope and size changes. The client changes the specifications for a project. The original proposal was to create fifty sales reports. Now the client wants an additional twenty-five reports with new data and parameters. The scope of the work has expanded, but the client maintains that it has not changed.

It would enrage most vendors that the client is unwilling to acknowledge the scope change. Their anger could manifest in the following two goals for negotiation:

- Goal 1: Prove to the client that the scope of the project has expanded.

This goal is shortsighted and lacks clarity. So the vendor proved he is right and the client is wrong. Where does he go from there? What is his target?

- Goal 2: Get compensation from the client for the additional reports.

Why is this narrow? It has a short-term focus. Does it solve the client's real problem? How does it help build a business relationship?

If the vendor's goal is to prove the client wrong or to make sure the client pays for changing demands, he or she is not going into negotiations with the right spirit. The vendor is going in with daggers, to win and to defeat the client.

The following goal for Scenario Two keeps the future of the relationship in mind.

- Goal 3: Set clear guidelines for project scope expansion or revisions.

This goal is beneficial to both sides because it sets clear future guidelines for the project, and the vendor is engaging the client in a discussion about both the current situation and a long-term solution.

Goals 1 and 2 in both scenarios, where the thought revolves around making the client pay, proving the client wrong, or compromising on quality, lead to an "I win, you lose" competitive situation.

Before finalizing the goal, the negotiator needs to answer these questions:

1. Do I have a common understanding of the problem with the client?
2. Do I know why the client is making these demands, so that I can address the cause rather than the symptoms? How can I understand what the client really needs?
3. Will the goal inspire the client to look for solutions for mutual benefit?
4. Will the goal give me an opportunity to strengthen our relationship?
5. Does this goal create a wall between the client and my company? (By *create a wall*, I mean creating an *us vs. them* mindset rather than the we approach.)
6. Is this goal achievable and measurable?

If you are not clear about the answers to these questions, it is better to go back to the drawing board.

REFLECT THE NEEDS OF BOTH SIDES

Don't give in all the time. Know why the client is making demands. If you are continually catering to their demands without knowing why they are making these demands, you will drain your resources, and the client may never be satisfied. If you get to the cause and come up with a solution that addresses the real need, not only is the client satisfied, but you are not exhausting your resources. You are positioning yourself as a problem-solver and partner to the client.

In Business Scenario One, the vendor has to understand the reason for budget cuts. Perhaps the client had lost a significant deal to a competitor? Maybe the client has identified a new vendor that promised to deliver the project at a lower price? When vendors react by catering to client demands, cutting project scope by 20 percent, or making them pay in other ways, they block the path to a good solution that addresses the needs of both sides.

A short-term focus or a reaction to requests will not help a vendor keep the client. Instead, the vendor needs to position himself as a problem-solver and a partner, and try to understand the client, the reasons for their demands, and come to an understanding with the client before engaging in negotiations.

USE *WE,* NOT *US VS. THEM*

The director of finance in a company refuses to fund projects considered critical by the head of marketing, because one manager in marketing had hurled insults at the finance department in prior meetings, and here's a chance to get even. Both lose sight of what is good for the company. The question to ask is, "Does my goal focus on defeating the other person? Am I using this negotiation to settle a personal score?" Sometimes the goal reflects the animosity between both sides, setting the tone and paving the way for such distractions as hidden agendas and personal attacks, with both teams losing sight of the business problem. What good can come out of a goal that will prove one person is right and the other person is wrong? This happens many times in negotiations.

DON'T LET THE WIN GO TO YOUR HEAD

The example of the book-balancing act illustrates what happens when the goal is personal and focuses on defeating the other person. It is not a business example, but a personal example sometimes creates a clearer visual and leaves a lasting impression on people. In a negotiation, goal setting is as critical as coming to a common understanding of the business problem.

Anita was in fourth grade. The school had a Sports Day every year when everyone took part in some competitive activity based on ability and interest. The fourth-grade teacher assigned the students who were not athletic to an insane book-balancing race. Anita was one of ten girls who took part in the race. The goal was to place a book on her head and, with arms spread wide to balance the book, walk to the finish line. Everyone had to use a history book. In every practice session, Rita, who was fast and competitive came out the winner. Since Rita and Anita were rivals in academics, she aimed to make Anita lose in the race, and she was vocal about it. Anita focused on balancing the book, so her goal was to keep the book from falling until she reached the finish line. She walked around the house with that odd book on her head, until she mastered the technique of keeping the book on her head for at least five minutes without falling.

On Sports Day, the ten girls were all on the start line. The whistle blew, and everyone started. When Anita got close to the finish line, Rita was ahead of her by a few feet. She turned around and looked at Anita, with the book in hand, and said, "I won. You lost." Anita still went forward with her book on her head to the finish line, because her goal was not about beating Rita to the finish line. Her goal was to finish with the book on her head. The referee disqualified Rita—she had taken the book off her head before she touched the finish line because she was busy proclaiming her win to Anita. Rita lost the race. Anita had to go on stage to receive the prize, which was a plastic water bottle with a red lid. Rita never spoke to Anita again. The water bottle was a constant reminder to

Anita to choose goals wisely. Outwitting others and proving them wrong should not be the driver for goal setting.

Choosing goals objectively without being jaded by likes and dislikes of the people involved in the business situation is challenging. But conscious effort and practice give you the discipline to choose a goal wisely, and stick to it throughout the negotiation. Eastern philosophy speaks extensively about personal likes and dislikes, and the negative outcomes one would encounter if swayed by strong likes and dislikes.

GETTING TO AN INSPIRED GOAL

The Adrift Website Case Study

Note: This case study of Paula's website-building journey illustrates key points of coming to a common understanding of the problem and practicing the Seven Rules.

Paula was a public speaker and instructor of management courses. She wanted a great-looking website to promote her business. Since the inception of her company, she had made several attempts, working with at least three vendors and spending significant money on designing a website. Somehow, the websites never did justice to her business. The site was unappealing and drew very little traffic.

She made one more attempt to redesign her website, but she was on a tight budget. She finally chose a vendor with some hesitation since the website design community had lost her trust.

The vendor submitted a proposal along with a tentative timeline. Paula accepted the proposal, which included three sample designs for the site, along with hosting details and content requirements. The website would have six pages, including a blog, animations on the first page, a client testimonial page, five videos linked to YouTube, ten photographs illustrating the different leadership workshops she offered, and links to Paula's social media accounts. Two weeks later, the vendor emailed Paula three sample designs. They arrived a day early, but Paula was not happy with the designs. She wanted to add more content, more pages, a new logo design, and more videos. Paula kept adding to her demands.

She had a long-term relationship with the website vendor and had even referred several major clients to them. The additional requirements would cost the vendor more time and staff resources, such as experts in logo design and social media. To the vendor's surprise, Paula did not even bring up the cost for the additional demands, so the vendor called Paula to set up a meeting to discuss the project—meaning, let us negotiate.

I discuss this Website Case Study in my classes on negotiation. At the beginning of the class, the participants answer the following questions, "If you were the vendor, would you comply with Paula's demands? Would you engage in a negotiation? What would be your goal?" These questions come before they learn the eight principles of negotiation—The Communications Signal and the Seven Rules.

Invariably, the answers from the class participants confirm that most negotiations start at the data or information stage and are all about the *us vs. them*, win-or-lose mindset, and contain goals with a narrow or short-term focus. As expected, the class labels Paula (the website client) as the villain in the whole situation. Here are the typical responses from class participants:

> The demands are unreasonable. We cannot accommodate these demands without more resources. We cannot meet her deadlines.

> If we do not comply, we may lose Paula as a client and lose future clients referred by her.

> We can prove that our sample designs meet the specifications approved by Paula in our original proposal. So, she has to pay for additions to her original specifications.

These statements are angry reactions. Their list of negotiation goals, in their role of a website designer, was no better.

> Double the price of our original quote.

> Ask Paula to withdraw new requirements and convince her to stick to the original proposal.

Ask Paula to meet us halfway.

Ask Paula to extend deadlines and resources.

Keep the client at all costs—comply or compromise and please the client.

These goals do not get to the heart of the problem. They are reactions to circumstances, and they reflect fears, desires, and an incorrect definition of the problem. Class participants playing the website designer role are taking a stand based on Paula's new demands.

Then the class learns the eight principles of negotiation. When the students reexamine the case study, they look at it with a fresh perspective and follow the path from Data to Insights. They review Paula's original Request For Proposal (RFP), her new website designer's proposal, her old website, statistics on traffic to her site, and the business relationship between the vendor and Paula. They carry out extensive discussions in their respective teams for the role-play and develop goals that have undoubtedly transformed. Participants in the classes are a mix of engineering, information technology (IT), marketing, and client-relations professionals, so the discussions are lively.

A common understanding of the problem is essential to set the goal for negotiation. Here is a description that combines the essence of the problem:

Description of the problem. Paula wanted the new website to look appealing and draw more traffic. The website designer came up with a proposal. She changed her original specifications. If the designer conforms to her new demands, the website will not differ from the previous ones. It will also cost a great deal more than budgeted, without yielding a positive outcome for either the client or the vendor. The business need for Paula was to create awareness in the market. Paula's specifications and her increasing demands are unlikely to address her business need, and to achieve increased market awareness for her services. The previous websites failed her because they focused on her training workshops and not her speaking ability, which set her apart from other training companies.

Based on the description of the problem, an inspired goal came from one team in the class:

New Inspired Goal. Create a website for Paula that will gain her the needed visibility as a public speaker without compromising our team's (the website designer's) business goals of adequate compensation and client retention. Paula's website will reflect, "Who she is and not just what she does." What sets Paula apart from other trainers is how powerful she is in public speaking.

The new goal is an inspired goal because it does not put the client and vendor on opposite teams. The problem definition and the goal show signs of looking inward and contemplating—What does the client need, not what does the client want? And, how can we match her need without hurting both of our budgets? The goal sustains both the vendor's and the client's strengths. It comes from an understanding of the problem and needs, and from seeing an opportunity to build a long-term relationship. The goal steers away from an *us vs. them* focus and takes the negotiation towards a *we* or one voice approach.

The right mindset determines a wise goal. As a client, Paula depends on the vendor to help her achieve her business goals. As already stated in chapter one, "What you do should protect and benefit the client. It implies that whatever you do, it should benefit you, too—you have to remain strong to protect your client."

Yielding to the client's desires or demands would weaken the vendor's income and resources. The goal also works from the vendor's point of view because it would strengthen the relationship with Paula and sustain business results. The key questions addressed by the goal:

Why does the client need a new website? Why did the prior sites fail in promoting her business?

How can we help Paula succeed in her business? How can we succeed—that is, expand awareness in the market for the client? What she needs is "her presence—her strong personality" on the website, so the viewers will get a sense of what she does, how well she does it, and how they could use her services.

We cannot claim we have helped Paula as a client unless she succeeds in her business with the help of the website.

How can we help the client realize that her specifications would not get her to her business goal? Past website designs did not gain her visibility in the market and did not set her apart from the many management trainers in the field.

The vendor, in this spirit, becomes Paula's business partner, a trusted advisor, and a consultant, rather than an order taker or profit monger. Even if the vendor had complied with all of Paula's requests, she might go back to them six months later complaining about a dysfunctional website. As website experts, they know how to help Paula achieve her business purpose without exceeding budget parameters.

This new goal would appeal to Paula as the website design client. As the client, Paula needed to establish her brand in the market and gain visibility as an expert. Her clients chose her because of her reputation as a speaker. Her previous websites failed her because she had hardly any traffic. The websites before did not leverage this strength; instead, they filled the pages with her workshops. She did not stand out from the many training firms that offered similar seminars. The additional pages, videos, and other demands made were just wants or desires that catered to her whims and fancies. These additions would not have brought her closer to the goal, because they focused on the services she provided and not on her brand as a powerful speaker. Paula had to perceive the website designer as creating value for her business.

There is no conflict of goals. Now that there is a clear goal that works for both parties, they can look at creative ways of reaching solutions.

If you're in a role similar to the website designer, here are typical questions you might ask to set your goals:

- Will the website address the client's business goals?
- What can we do to make our client stand out from her competition?
- Do the client's new demands help her achieve the goals?
- Do we have the expertise to accommodate her need for image building?
- Have we done similar websites that can serve as a prototype for the client?

Now, when the vendor proposes arguments, alternatives, and outcomes, it will be with the spirit of partnership—we win if you succeed in your goal. The vendor adjusts the entire proposal with this goal in mind; this will create value for both the vendor and Paula—a value-path for success. This outcome should be the focus throughout the negotiation process. It changes the tone of the meeting.

FOCUS ON NEEDS

What is the difference between needs, opportunity, and desires? Why can't we focus on what the client desires? Eastern philosophy distinguishes between desires and needs. Desires or wants are self-gratifying. You satisfy one desire and another crops up almost instantaneously. It is as insatiable as a craving for chocolates for someone who loves chocolates! Think about Paula's *desires*.

- I want my website to have bright colors.
- I want my website to have many pages to give the impression I have an array of services and a long list of clients.
- I want people to listen to all my videos.
- Why not post all my articles? Why do I have to condense them?
- I want to show more workshops on my website than my competition.

Paula is telling the vendor what to do, and the average vendor will only take a stand. Let us look at how vendors react to *desires*.

- Prove that our designs meet Paula's specifications.
- We are right and Paula is wrong.
- Get more money from Paula. Ask for more time.
- Let us expand the scope of Paula's project.

Ego drives desires or wants and can lead to both sides taking a stand and bargaining, where one has to lose for another to win. You want what you want, and you might think there is no reason you should not have it.

What does she *need?* To promote her business so she can achieve her revenue goals. When you base a negotiation goal on a business need, you can leverage an opportunity to benefit both parties. In this situation, the foundation for negotiation is your long-term goal, where the larger purpose and your relationship with the other person overshadow your immediate gains or losses. This approach reassures the other person that you care about his or her interests, too, and you are not there for the "kill." Desires lead to competing techniques, while the situation here is to work with consensus and not by competing.

YOUR GUIDE TO RULE I

Ask yourself these questions:

1. Do we have a shared understanding of the problem?
2. Does the goal address the needs of both sides?

3. Is the goal driven by desires?
4. Is the goal designed to prove the other side wrong?
5. Is the goal influenced by an intention to outwit the other person or even a personal score?

CHAPTER FIVE

RULE II.
ASK WHAT, NOT WHO

WHERE ARE WE?

No strategy can help if people approach business negotiations with a short-term focus on winning rather than building a long-term relationship. Also, timing is everything. A common understanding of the problem and establishing a wise goal are required to proceed with any negotiation. The remaining six rules support the negotiator's intention to strengthen long-term relationships and business results. Rule II, *Ask What, Not Who*, is critical to building harmony in relationships (see Figure 8).

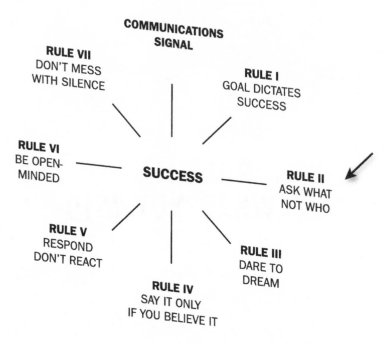

FIGURE 8. Rule II: The *Chakra* of Negotiation Principles.

ELEMENTS OF RULE II

- Look Through Process Lens
- No Finger-Pointing Artists
- Make All Part of the Solution
- Show Attitude of Gratitude

LOOK THROUGH PROCESS LENS

Have you ever worked in a place where every team task was a success, and no problems ever occurred? Negotiation revolves around business problems. If you think people caused them, then your focus is on the people, and you cannot solve the problems. So, Rule II is guiding you to shift your attention away from people and toward the problem. You may have heard variations of this rule in the workplace. My first exposure to this principle happened when I began my change management journey in the 1990s.

Every work environment has seen some blunders. These could be simple typos in emails or broadcasting the wrong marketing message to customers. Here, the focus is not on how big or small the blunder could be, but on how people can shift the lens of their attention to the problem or the process instead of the people. Figure out what the problem is and how to solve it, rather than who caused the problem and how to make them pay for it. No matter how far companies have progressed in technology and science, whenever an issue crops up, people settle into old ways and blame others. Even high-performing teams can end up getting paranoid and visibly frustrated with a situation. They begin the never-ending finger-pointing game. We, as humans, look for external causes to blame for our botches.

NO FINGER-POINTING ARTISTS

The *Case of a Confused Mailing* illustrates what happens when you try to blame someone for a business problem and how you can turn it around with a different mindset.

Tricia was the marketing manager for a division of a financial company. The head of the division decided to withdraw an old financial product from the market and replace it with two alternative product offerings. The old product was an administrative nightmare. The customers could make the switch to one of the two new alternatives at the time of their annual renewal. However, the results of a market research study showed that one customer segment was not happy about product withdrawal and wanted to keep the old product. The division decided to send a mailing to the remaining customer segments announcing the withdrawal of the old financial product. Vanessa, the marketing analyst in Tricia's team, requested the database team to generate mailing labels for customers enrolled in the old product. Vanessa instructed them to exclude the customer segment that wanted to keep the old financial product. Mailings went out like clockwork.

All hell broke loose a week later when customer complaints flooded the phone lines. The customer segment that was supposed to be excluded from the mailing received the announcements. Everyone involved in sending the mailing devoted time to finding out "who dun it?" The IT and operations divisions pointed out some mistakes in the marketing analyst's instructions. They asked marketing to pay for resource time to fix the problems. There was no shared understanding of what had happened. They had several crisis meetings, and every time, the team members took up the age-old blame game—not my fault, you did it—until it reached the C-suite two weeks after the mailing.

The head of the marketing division, Kevin, was a big proponent of change management. Tricia reported to Kevin. He told Tricia privately that he would not want to shoulder the entire cost of fixing the problem, and he would like her to negotiate a fifty-fifty budget split. To his disappointment, she failed!

MAKE ALL PART OF THE SOLUTION

Kevin believed in making everyone part of the solution. He intervened and brought the team managers from marketing, operations, IT, customer research, and customer service into a conference room. Everyone went armed with facts and figures. It was a hostile crowd. Kevin's opening statements threw all of them off- guard.

Here's the gist of what he said:

Team, I am very impressed with the quality of your work. We received positive comments from many customers eager to switch to the new product. You all pooled together to launch this mailing. Customer research was right on the mark. Marketing, hats off to you for the creative work.

Let us thank customer service for alerting us to the customer complaints. IT and operations, I am surprised you generated mailing labels early and executed the mailing. Congratulations! It was teamwork at its best. Now, let us see how we can put the same enthusiasm into fixing the problem and putting in a process to avert future mishaps. Let us retrace our steps and focus on what went wrong. Next, determine what role each of us could play in fixing it.

Boy, did he redefine the problem with a solution in mind. The problem is not that the mailing went to the blocked customers. Reassuring angry customers and preventing future such mishaps were the real problems. Phew, what a relief! He shifted the focus from the blame game to customer satisfaction. He then turned to Pat and said, "You are the customer research expert, good at moderating discussions, why don't you take over from here? I have another meeting. I will be back in one hour and look forward to the answers."

· · · · · · · · · ·

THE TEAM LEARNED TWO ADDITIONAL LESSONS

- Define the problem with solutions in mind.
- Acknowledge people's work or contributions.

· · · · · · · · · ·

Kevin's acknowledgment of teamwork gave everyone a sense of ownership. Everyone realized that people worked hard to make the mailing a success. Mistakes can happen, and when they do, you cannot take away the contributions made by individuals by blaming them. They will have no incentive to put in extra effort in future projects. The team understood, and the language changed from "you did it" to "we did it!" They spent the next hour focusing on the "what and why," and not the "who." The team came to a common understanding of the problem. There was a disconnect in the way the marketing and IT departments defined customer segments—marketing and IT departments did not speak the same language. They selected a liaison that would translate business requirements to the IT department for future marketing projects.

The team found a creative solution for stemming the immediate loss and avoiding similar future mishaps. They redirected their effort toward developing a strategy for calming angry customers. The entire team made calls to those customers to explain the error.

Eastern philosophy gives us the teaching: you create the world around you. Your surroundings are not the cause of your problems. How you perceive it is the problem. Take ownership and look inward for the solutions.

SHOW ATTITUDE OF GRATITUDE

The confusion in the mailing was not any one person's fault. Redefining the problem, shifting the focus from people and blame to problem and process, conveying gratitude, and acknowledging good work changed the tone of the meeting and yielded positive results. Marketing and IT analysts worked on how to give specifications and how to define lead times, checkpoints, roles, and responsibilities. Not that everyone had a foolproof system, but they knew how to team up, dive in, and fix problems. Accountability matters, but not in the blame game!

After hearing the customer-mailing story, questions that arise in the minds of listeners show the doubts in their mainstream minds:

What if we start with gratitude, and the client thinks, "Okay, I am right, they are wrong," and that is why they are grateful and conciliatory?

I have proof that the client is at fault. I could use this in my favor. Why waste time with gratitude?

It may come back to haunt us. What if the clients think we are faking it? Sometimes nice doesn't work.

"Nice doesn't hurt, either." An essential ingredient in any meeting is tone. If you set a pleasant mood, you are removing the noise in everyone's heads so they can focus on the real issues and not on emotions. Having worked in many industries and companies, ranging from small businesses to multinationals, I can say with confidence that nice works, and politeness pays. People are people.

FOCUS ON THE PROBLEM AND SHOW GRATITUDE

The Adrift Website Case Study

It's impressive to see how quickly attendees of my classes on negotiation adapt to the attitude of gratitude. In class role-plays, the team spokesperson kicks off the discussion by thanking each team member from the client or vendor side for a specific contribution. It sets the tone. No negotiation tool or technique will work if the mood of the meeting is contentious.

Getting back to the Adrift Website Case Study where Paula is the client, and the vendor is a website designer. In the initial role-play, before exposure to this rule, "Ask what, not who," and the customer mailing story, participants in the negotiation classes focused on gathering evidence to prove the client wrong, to show that Paula's new demands were not part of the original requirements and that any extra costs and delays were not the vendor's fault.

After listening to the mass-mailing story, the class participants stopped blaming Paula for unreasonable demands. Instead, they focused on redefining the problem, shifting their focus to the process, and expressing gratitude for Paula's business.

They stopped perceiving Paula's demands as unreasonable and focused on the problem: "Paula was not happy with her past website because it brought no traffic. Her website did not focus on her strengths, her powerful presence as a leader and a communicator. It focused on training products and services."

One vendor team in a class role-play created a revised proposal to make the website meet Paula's business goals without sacrificing the vendor's purpose. The proposal included sample websites of two well-known public speakers whose sites attracted a record number of visitors. The team created mock web pages for Paula's website that looked similar to the two public speakers' websites. It brought out Paula's power as a speaker and differentiated her from the other firms that offered identical workshops. Anyone visiting her website would know why they should choose Paula as their trainer or coach for public speaking. The vendor team in the role-play concluded, "We are glad to be working with you, Paula. Your business success is our goal. You connect so well with your audience in the videos. Let us bring your talent to the forefront on the website. Our whole team is excited and has worked hard to create this proposal for you." Such sweet words would be music to Paula's ears.

Finger-pointing is an art perfected by some people, and the corporate culture in some companies nurtures it. Don't become finger-pointing artists. Take ownership. Ask the questions: what caused this situation, what is the solution, and what role can I play in reaching this solution? When you take ownership of the problem, you can take ownership of the solution. You cannot solve a problem for which you blame yourself or someone else. Anger, guilt, and fear of repercussions cloud your mind, and you cannot come to a common understanding of the problem. The other person is going through similar emotions. Ownership does not mean assuming blame. It means taking responsibility.

YOUR GUIDE TO RULE II

Ask yourself these questions:

1. Are we defining the problem with a solution in mind?
2. Why did it occur? What went wrong? *Not*, who did it?
3. What role can we each play to resolve the problem?
4. Have I acknowledged work by people on both sides?
5. Did I say Thank You?

CHAPTER SIX

RULE III.
DARE TO DREAM

WHERE ARE WE?

Rule II showed the benefit of directing your attention to the problem rather than pointing the finger at people who could have caused the problem. You now learn that you cannot solve the problem if you expect the worst to happen. Rule III in this chapter *Dares You To Dream* (See Figure 9).

FIGURE 9. Rule III: The *Chakra* of Negotiation Principles.

ELEMENTS OF RULE III

- Expect the Best
- Common Fears
- Combat Fears
- Fear Equals *Us vs. Them*

EXPECT THE BEST

A successful negotiation is a careful examination of the situation to find a solution that serves the needs of both parties intending to build long-term relationships. How can you develop a relationship if fears and preconceived negative notions about the other person torment you? Dreams, hopes, and intentions, not fears, influence the positive outcomes of a negotiation.

COMMON FEARS

Fears fall under four categories: outcomes, cooperation, conflicts, and failure. Here are some statements or questions associated with each of the four categories. You may have heard them before. When you hear a person make these statements or ask these questions, you know what type of fear is assailing them, and you can take that into consideration during negotiations.

FEAR OF OUTCOME

- What will happen to me?
- I will lose my client if I say no to their demands.
- I may lose my job if I keep asking my boss for more resources to comply with client demands.
- I feel like a loser when the client is upset, even if I get my way in negotiations.

FEAR OF A LACK OF SUPPORT

- Support teams will refuse to cooperate with new client requests.
- Management will refuse to give more resources.
- How do I work with clients when we don't see eye-to-eye on what they want?

FEAR OF CONFLICTS

- I am not good at dealing with conflicts.
- How can I negotiate without being confrontational?
- The head of the division does not like my boss. It is not going to be easy to discuss with the head of the division.
- He always gets his way in meetings because he is loud and offensive.

FEAR OF FAILURE

- Nothing works. Tried them all. Good ideas, but they failed before.
- I don't like disappointments, so I go in preparing for the worst.
- My new project is doomed. Last year two leaders who took on that project either quit or lost their jobs.

These are defeatist attitudes, which don't bode well for long-term relationships. You are reacting to images you or others have created in your mind.

COMBAT FEARS

How can you handle such fears? The same way you combat your fear of taking the SAT, GRE, and other entrance exams: prepare and practice until you perfect it. Be positive. The examples in this chapter show how fear can inhibit progress, and what you can do to gain a more positive attitude. The experiences of four people show ways you can overcome fears.

TRAPPED IN THE MIDDLE SEAT

What happens when you fear outcomes and lack of cooperation? The one thing that made Lisa nervous about flights was the seating arrangements. She dreaded the thought of sitting in the middle seat, even if it was a half-hour flight. For one business trip, Lisa had made reservations with an international airline that does not give seat assignments when you buy the ticket. You only get to reserve the seat twenty-four hours before the trip. She was resigned to canceling the trip if the airline assigned her a seat in the middle.

She was thinking about the insanity of this twenty-four-hour rule and was angry when she called the airline a week before the trip. Her goal: "I want an aisle seat. I don't want to sit in the middle seat." She started the conversation with the agent by expressing her fear of the middle seat proclaiming that she would have to cancel the trip if she did not get an aisle or window seat. She also called this rule ridiculous and compared them to other airlines. Sure enough, the agent refused to give her a seat since it was a week before the trip. In a disapproving tone, the agent said, "If everyone refuses to sit in the middle seat, what can we do? Most window and aisle seats are taken."

Lisa confided in her friend, "Oh my God, I am doomed. If I get a middle seat, I will cancel the trip. I will lose the money and perhaps the client too. The airline couldn't care less." The thought of a long trip seated between two passengers paralyzed her. Her friend said, "Lisa, where is your positive attitude? You have already decided your fate. You will get an aisle seat. Why don't you call the airline again and talk to an agent? Each agent is different. Go with a smile. Don't do it online, though."

The next morning, after a brisk walk, Lisa called the airline with the positive thought: "They will figure out a way to get me an aisle seat." She even pictured herself in a reclining seat. She expressed her need to sit in an aisle seat for this business trip and told the agent she knew this airline would figure out a way for her, a loyal customer. The agent put her on hold and returned with something that was music to her ears: "Ma'am, business-class seats are available. I see that you are a premium mileage customer and you have more miles than needed. We could accommodate you. Are you willing to use mileage?"

Willing? She was ready to scream with joy and would have paid cash to get it! When you go with a positive, calm attitude and a conciliatory tone, while expecting the best, you make it easier for others to want to think of better alternatives. You will not be saying things that would make the other person take a stand. There are no guarantees, but you increase your odds of success.

After hearing the story, someone asked, "What if there were no business class seats?" When you are in a dream, do you worry about the details or ask how the dream will come true? The dream is an inspiration, and you cannot kill it with the mechanics. In this airline scenario, the agent may have come up with other alternatives. Your job is to be positive and inspire creativity. Stop seeing intentions behind people's actions. The enemy exists in your mind—we create a monster out of the situation or the people on the "other side." The airline is not out to get Lisa—they are not trapping her in the middle seat!

If you can delude yourself into imagining the worst, you can use the same mind to visualize the best outcomes.

NOTHING WORKS. TRIED THEM ALL

Many people express fear of outcomes before they ask for a salary increase, a promotion, or a transfer to another department. Some even fear to present new ideas for projects. They miss golden opportunities for negotiation. What are the reasons for such thoughts? The memory of past negative experiences, stories of failed attempts by colleagues, and anxiety about outcomes block their minds. Are you familiar with these pessimistic thoughts?

- I tried asking for a promotion last year and got a slap on the wrist.
- The boss pointed out my mistakes more frequently.
- My colleague, who approached my boss for a transfer, became a target when layoffs happened.
- The head of our department has a reputation for blocking staff transfers to other divisions, so why should I try asking?
- I rarely make suggestions in meetings because my manager is very insecure and insults people who bring up new ideas.

Such perceived outcomes are fertile grounds for failure. Even if they are true, you fail when you give up. If you are content with your present state, there is no problem. When such fears paralyze people into inaction or drive them to incorrect action, I can see a "dis-ease" state, which absorbs every aspect of their careers. When they operate out of such fears, they may leave a trail of mistakes. Don't let the fear of adverse reactions move you into inaction. Take the driver's seat, take stock of your past accomplishments and the field of possibilities ahead of you. Identify your strengths and drivers for success, and present your case or idea with a positive thought for both the listener and for yourself.

A technique that works like magic is the Accomplishment Grid. You create a grid of your top ten accomplishments in the past five years. They can include work, school, or other extracurricular activities like volunteer work or sports. It never ceases to amaze me how everyone feels good after this exercise. Do it before you step into negotiations.

Accomplishment Grid

Brief Description	Goals Achieved	Who did it benefit? How did it benefit?	What made you accomplish?	Your two strengths that helped you accomplish

Jennifer was unhappy in her job because her manager took every opportunity to put her down and made a point to not include her in any of the major initiatives or meetings. Her meetings with her boss concluded in her ideas being shot down, and her requests for additional resources or training denied. Her self-confidence had reached a low ebb. In one of those "impulsive moments," she asked to meet with the head of the department to "complain." She then panicked and reached out to me. We went through defining the problem, setting the goal for the meeting, and completing this

Accomplishment Grid. By the time she completed the fifth accomplishment, she had regained her feeling of self-worth. Her meeting with the department head was about how she loved the company, the leadership, her team, what she has accomplished, and what she could bring to the table if given a chance. The department head assigned her to a new project.

Dare to dream. If you are asking for a promotion, start with how you enjoy working in the unit, how management's encouragement has boosted your development, and how you see yourself performing with a promotion—something that will make you and your boss look good. Why not? Even if you don't get the promotion right away, your request leaves your boss thinking about it more favorably and they may not perceive your aspirations as a potential threat.

FEAR EQUALS *US VS. THEM*

People sometimes express the following "doom and gloom" statements about their clients:

- The clients want to squeeze more work out of us.
- We have to give in or fight them.
- They are our bosses, and most of their demands are unreasonable and sometimes unnecessary.
- We are helpless because we cannot change the clients' business practices.
- It has become our way of life in business.

If you have such thoughts about clients, ask yourself these questions:

- Why do I see evil intentions behind client demands?
- Why are demands perceived as orders? Is the client's wish my command?
- If I keep giving in because of what I perceive as the client's intentions or reactions, will I not exhaust my resources and become weaker?
- When do I reach a point where I say "No more?"

If you continue moving ahead with the fear of losing the client, you will not expand your thinking or find a common path to explore creative solutions with clients.

Combat fear with courage. Fear expresses an *us vs. them* mindset. When you are afraid, it means that you are focused on yourself. Others take a back seat. You ask yourself, "Oh, what will happen to me? How can I protect myself?"

With courage comes the confidence to think of others. You ask, "What is the client's real need? How can I preserve this business relationship?" You dare to dream. Clients may keep ordering, even if their demands do not meet their goals. Will you keep on taking the orders? Remember, Paula could keep adding to the Adrift website even if the site did not need the features. Dare to look beyond client demands and see what you can do to benefit them.

WILL I LOSE THE CONTRACT?

Marina is an independent consultant working in management training. A prospective client wanted her to do a brief demo of her training class for the managers in the learning and development team. They liked her and were ready to sign the contract. The income potential was huge for Marina. However, her training was not conducive to a half-hour demo. It was all or nothing. She would have to do a demo of the entire two-hour class for it to make sense. The training materials were proprietary, and a means for her livelihood. Her mentor, business partners, and friends were firmly in favor of the demo. They said, "Marina if you don't do the demo, you lose the prospective client. They will give you a big project with high-income potential. It is a huge amount to sacrifice. It is a common business practice to ask for a demo, and you have to take such risks to get your foot in the door."

Marina sought the help of a consultant who asked her, "How do you feel about the demo? Is your fear of losing the prospective client greater than your fear of losing your IP [intellectual property]? Does the earning potential cover the loss of your IP? Is this your dream client?"

Marina concluded that the dream of reaching out to many clients with her training was more exciting than making money from this one client. The consultant then said to Marina, "You created this program, and you enjoy every time you deliver it. It is your dream. If you did the demo, it would be out of fear of losing a prospective client. Hold on to your dream. Talk frankly with the prospect, present an alternative with confidence, and share your excitement about doing the program for them that would bring a positive change in their employees. Explain to them it is your company practice not to do demos. Ask them to sign a contract with you, which will protect your rights and provide payment for the first training class. If they are happy with your program, they can hire you for the thirty sessions. If your program does not meet their expectations, then their only loss is the payment for one session."

The prospect became a client, and Marina did several sessions. She concluded that she does better when she doesn't let fear drive her decisions. People can sense fear and may take advantage of you when you express it. That does not mean that people have bad intentions and are out to get you. Each of us wants to do the best for our project team or company, and if we can get the other person to play along, why not?

A POSITIVE ATTITUDE LEADS TO SUCCESS

The Adrift Website Case Study

How can you achieve the goal if you think you will lose in the negotiation or lose the client? In one of my negotiation classes, one team played the role of the website designer, and the other team played the role of Paula, the client. The team playing the role of the website designer went with a positive mindset into negotiations with Paula for redesigning the Adrift Website. Their new mindset was, "We are the experts, and our client will see the value in our suggestions for her business success." This mindset will pave the path for success in the relationship, and more alternatives will present themselves with this intention.

When you listen to inspirational speeches, you are more likely to go into negotiations with a positive attitude. After listening to the speech of an inspirational leader, each participant in my class wrote one positive outcome from the negotiation with Paula. The best suggestion for an outcome came from a person new to negotiations, "Paula recommends us to a major client because her income has doubled." Such an elevated thought raises the level of the negotiation, injects creativity, and helps you steer clear of pettiness.

Before you embark on any negotiation, listen to inspirational talks by great leaders—I am partial to the commencement speech delivered by the late Steve Jobs, past chairman, chief executive officer, and co-founder of Apple Inc., in 2005 for the graduating class at Stanford University. Everyone must have a favorite. The inspirational talks help cut out the harmful noise in one's head and any lingering pettiness. It puts you on a higher level of thinking and shifts your attention to those that achieved the impossible. You will gain the courage to combat any fears. If that doesn't do it for you, consider music, a brisk walk, or anything else that can help you dream big. Why should you deny yourself the dream just because the world says so?

You need to put yourself on a higher plane to get past negative thoughts and pettiness. You are not dealing with buildings, structures, and entities; you are dealing with people, who are not out to get you. Instead, they want to work with you. It's not about them. It's about you! All you can do is prepare yourself. This is an important aspect of Eastern philosophy, which teaches the benefits of looking at the world from inside out. When you perceive yourself as the product of external influences, you spend your time trying in vain to change the surrounding people rather than looking within to see how you can change yourself to be successful in the existing environment.

Often, we forget how important it is to set the mood for business discussions. Hope, dreams, and intention set the mood. Don't let the fear of someone's intention dictate your responses. Get inspired! Dare to dream. Soon you will live that dream.

YOUR GUIDE TO RULE III

Ask yourself these questions:

1. How does fear help me?
2. Why would anyone have evil intentions toward me?
3. What would be the outcome, if I expected the worst to happen in negotiations?
4. So what if I have tried and failed before?
5. What is wrong with dreaming big?

CHAPTER SEVEN

RULE IV.
SAY IT ONLY IF
YOU BELIEVE IT

WHERE ARE WE?

The negotiator has reached a common understanding of the problem with the client, set the goal for success, and recognizes the need to focus on issues when difficult situations surface during negotiations, and the importance of intentions, hopes, and dreams in achieving the goal. The next rule shows what happens when people speak without conviction (see Figure 10).

FIGURE 10. Rule IV: The *Chakra* of Negotiation Principles.

ELEMENTS OF RULE IV

- Credibility Matters
- Are You Persuasive?
- Confident or Confused Speaker
- Commitment or Crutch Words

CREDIBILITY MATTERS

What gives credibility is the conviction with which you present yourself in negotiations. How can you show confidence if you don't believe in the goal or the solutions to the business problem?

Believe in what you are saying. If you don't, why should anyone else? Put the passion in the belief and express it with confidence and conviction. This advice applies equally well to speaking and to negotiation.

This kind of confidence comes from a space of integrity. It is not something people can get through training or coaching. They cannot pretend to believe or to be confident. The audience can see through the pretense. Integrity creates credibility with the audience. If a vendor starts his or her pitch in the meeting with, "Here are two options for solving the business problem or addressing the business opportunity; I *think* both will work," the client will not have confidence in those options. If the vendor only "thinks" the two options will work, why should the client even consider the options during a negotiation? Instead, the client will offer counter options.

But does "I think" always reflect uncertainty? Some use the phrase when they don't want people to think they are pushy or overconfident. Whether you can say, "I think" depends on the circumstance. If an analyst is presenting the results of a market research study to decision-makers, she cannot say, "I think our market share dropped by 10 percent." That will raise questions about the validity of the study. Instead, the analyst has to make sure the data supports her conclusions and then convey the message with confidence so that the audience can take action. If you present two alternative solutions to a client while negotiating, do it only if you think the solutions would work. And, don't diminish the value of your options by showing any uncertainty.

So, when can you use the phrase, "I think"? If a colleague asks you for your opinion on a project, and you don't have all the facts, you can say, "I think the project is going well." You are softening your opinion so that your colleague will not rely entirely on you to make her decisions.

Or, if someone in your team is waiting for your suggestions and if you are grooming him to be a manager, you want to tone down your statements so you don't disempower him or make him dependent on you to decide. You can tell your team member, "I think this is the right approach for the project. What do you think?"

It is best not to make it a practice to use "I think" intending to please others; "I think" has to be used when the circumstance warrants it.

People remember the tone behind a speaker's words. They rarely remember the words. Belief is what the speaker feels—words are a reflection.

ARE YOU PERSUASIVE?

Have you ever wondered what the impact of being persuasive is in business meetings and negotiations? What would happen if a person does not speak with conviction in a business meeting to negotiate the annual budget for his department? The head of the marketing division asked Gary to represent him in an executive session to negotiate budget allocation for marketing. The head of the division put together a list of ten large projects based on prior years' requests. He told Gary, "The goal is to get $1.5 million in funding. Here is the list of proposed projects for next year. These are the projects we did last year. So, go for it."

One look at the list convinced Gary that five of the projects were no longer needed or relevant. "Don't worry, Gary," the division head said. "The goal is to get the budget. We can later use the budget for other critical projects."

Blissfully ignorant of the budget allocation process, Gary walked into the meeting—or shall we say, into a trap! Gary went in without a common understanding of the situation with the executives in the meeting. He had no confidence in the options he presented to get the budget. The executives gave him a tough fight. Although his company respected him as a marketing expert, Gary could not persuade the executive team to fund any of the five projects considered irrelevant, since he had doubts about the need for them.

Gary realized this line of discussion did not bode well for his department's credibility or relationship with the executive team. Finally, he apologized and said that he did not come prepared and asked them if they would give him another chance to revise the list based on their needs. He made this appeal with such conviction that the executive team yielded to his request. As he left, Gary made a promise to himself that he would never get into negotiation and present options if he had doubts about them. How could he convince the executives if he himself would not have funded the five projects?

Clara was a market analyst in a bank, and experienced positive results when she was persuasive. Her research showed that the market ranked her bank lower than the competition, a three-year downward trend accompanied by a slow erosion of business. Performance of the bank's ancillary products contributed to this low ranking. Some digging led her to the conclusion that her bank had some catching up to do on these ancillary products. Sales staff had expertise in the traditional products but lacked comfort in selling or servicing new ancillary products. Her boss asked Clara, "Are you sure about this, Clara? We will take a big risk if we are wrong. Our bank is investing the bulk of its resources on refining traditional products. Also, your research is asking us to dedicate resources to ancillary products."

"I am dead sure," she said. "I have the data, and I trust my analysis. Experts in the research firm validated the results.

Here is data…" Clara spoke with such conviction her boss put her in front of a room full of senior sales executives, who challenged her conclusions. Clara's convincing presentation was the beginning of a new sales program—hiring, training, and resourcing for ancillary products.

Gary's budget allocation meeting and Clara's presentation are examples of what happens in negotiations when you believe in what you are saying, and you have data to back that up.

Why do people listen to some great speakers and come away with decisive action steps? It is because the speakers' passion moves the audience.

Many clients put aside options presented by vendors or consultants if they are even remotely doubtful about project deliverables. Before offering options in negotiations, ask this critical question, "Would I accept these options, if I were in the client's shoes?" It is a litmus test for believability. If your answer is No Way, Don't Know, or Not Sure, go back to the drawing board. A lack of believability is where many negotiations fail.

A CONVINCING PROPOSAL

The Adrift Website Case Study

An inspired goal for negotiation came from a team that played the role of the vendor in one of my classes. The goal was to create a website for the client, Paula, that will help her gain visibility without compromising the team's (that is, the vendor's) business goals of adequate compensation and client retention. The website will reflect who Paula is and not just what she does.

Each vendor team in the role-play presented their proposal to the class. The rest of the class played the role of Paula, the client, in these team exercises. One team came back with a proposal they knew would win Paula over because the options they presented aligned with the inspired goal of the negotiation. They approached their work by remembering the rule, "Goal dictates success."

They presented two sample mock-up designs of Paula's website; sample one complied with all her demands, and the second addressed the goal of gaining Paula visibility, making her the focus. The contrast in the two examples was glaring. Without saying it openly, they showed how Paula's demands would keep her away from achieving her goal of publicity. The second sample was impressive because they backed their proposal with a demo of another popular speaker's website and showed stats on how that speaker gained visibility. The team playing the role of website designer asked the audience to imagine Paula's content on this website. Imagine a real estate agent taking you to a house where you can visualize yourself living with comfort. The vendor's enthusiasm overcame all the objections from the audience who played the role of Paula.

Sometimes words cannot describe your message, and you may need the support of visuals as with Paula's website, where they created the image of Paula as a great speaker.

They met the goal for the negotiation and laid the foundation for a long-term relationship.

CONFIDENT OR CONFUSED SPEAKER

Getting to the point and being precise in your responses keeps the negotiations clean. Some people use long-winded sentences with no pause, leaving the listener to figure out the answer or think the speaker either doesn't know the answer or is hiding the truth. Sometimes listeners get frustrated and pick on every word uttered by the speaker, prolonging negotiation meetings. Don't leave room for speculation—get to the point.

Frank was giving a presentation on the results of company-wide customer satisfaction research to senior executives of four divisions representing the individual market and small, medium, and large business markets. The results were critical for the senior executives to prioritize resources within their divisions. After prioritizing, they had to engage in extensive negotiations with the chief financial officer for budget allocation. If the division shifted its budget to improve customer service because the customer satisfaction ratings were low, then they risked losing the budget for sales initiatives. It was all about trade-offs.

Frank was an expert in analytics. He had sliced the data every which way he could with advanced statistical applications. The overall satisfaction scores were low. Someone in the audience said, "I am surprised at the low score. Does the sample include small business customers? I thought they liked us."

Frank hesitated before he replied. "Hmm, let me see. I think so. It has to be on the list you sent because every division gave the list directly to the survey firm and not to us. I requested you to send a list that represented your entire customer base. You know, we don't have access to the list, *you* do, and we have no way of checking the lists. The research firm selected a random sample from your list." It was a long-winded sentence that made the audience angry. They shouted out questions at Frank, leaving him flustered. "Frank, what do you mean 'you think so?' If you did not include small business in the survey, what are we doing here? Is it not your responsibility to check? You are the analyst."

The ranting went on until one of the other analysts on his team asked Frank to check Slide 20, which had sampling data. Frank then said, "It looks like the survey included small business." *Looks like—that is not very reassuring!* After this exchange, the audience questioned him on every point he made.

A simple response would have preserved his credibility: "The original research design included all market segments. I will confirm it for you." Another point to consider: in a meeting, you don't want to point fingers or deflect. Go for the neutral answer. Frank's original response implied, "If the survey did not include small business customers, it is your fault—not mine." If you don't know the answer, say so.

If you are precise and clear, you send out a signal of confidence to everyone involved in the negotiation.

COMMITMENT OR CRUTCH WORDS

It is advisable to use commitment phrases that show confidence. When a speaker uses commitment words, he or she gives the perception of being in charge. If you believe in what you are saying, you use words that show your commitment. At the first sign of crutch words, the audience will doubt you. If you lean heavily on a crutch, they suspect that you are hiding some problem or you are trying not to say what you honestly feel or want to convey.

Commitment phrases include words that inspire trust and confidence in the speaker's ability to assume responsibility. Crutch words leave the listener with some doubts about the speaker or what he or she is trying to say. It doesn't mean that a speaker cannot ever use crutch words. It just means that if crutch words are used frequently, it raises doubts in the listener's mind.

COMMITMENT WORDS AND PHRASES

- Yes, I will get back to you.
- I don't know.
- I am not sure.
- I will look into it.
- Absolutely. Unquestionably.

- I can do it, without a doubt.
- No.

You probably can come up with many more commitment phrases that make you say, "She knows what she is saying. I may not agree with what she says, but she is upfront, and her message is clear." But, you don't want to mislead the audience by saying, "Absolutely, I will do it," when you don't mean it.

CRUTCH WORDS AND PHRASES

People use crutch words and phrases when they are:

- Nervous about speaking up in a meeting
- Afraid of offending someone
- Intimidated by persons of authority (boss, executives, clients)
- Not sure how to answer a question
- Don't have the answer and don't want to admit to it
- Afraid to share bad news
- Hiding the facts—avoiding or deflecting the issue

Examples of crutch words and sounds:

- Hmm...
- Like, you know
- Perhaps, possibly, probably, maybe

- I think
- However, and, because (when used more than once in a sentence)
- Too many awkward pauses, coughing, clearing of the throat

The first two crutch sounds and phrases are sometimes a force of habit and hard to break. A nervous person uses these more frequently. None of these phrases by themselves raise doubts. Everyone uses them. However, when anyone uses these phrases frequently while sharing critical data or answering specific questions in a negotiation to influence decisions, then it confuses people or raises a red flag. It is better to get to the point and try not to lean on crutch words.

Imagine a vendor is answering a question posed by a client in a negotiation meeting.

The client asks, "Why would it take six weeks to add a few new requirements to the project?"

Vendor replies, "*You know*, it is not a few *because* you are asking us to add five new requirements and they are not small changes. Our technical team *thinks* each one *might* take two full weeks for making changes *and* our quality assurance team needs additional time for testing. We also added some time for your input and approval after changes. We have to double staff levels to do the job, and our cost estimate for the project increased."

Run-on sentences during project discussions with clients are not uncommon, but it is not the way to convince clients. It would be simpler to show a chart with calculations and say to the client, "Our technical team came up with the estimates. This chart shows how they came up with the estimate. We are open to any ideas that may bring down costs. Let us discuss."

If you are brief in your answers, it opens up a dialogue in place of the monologue. When you use long sentences and express different thoughts, then the answer escapes the audience. In negotiation, it is vital to look the other person straight in the eye, take pauses, and be brief about what you are saying. Let the other person ask you questions. Don't give lengthy explanations—they come out sounding like excuses, rather than reasons.

Go for your gut feeling. If you don't feel right about an option you are presenting to a client, the client will not feel good about it either. It shows in your speech and body language. The client can see the invisible crutch.

Some cultures are more prone to using crutch words while conversing with people of authority. You cannot conclude that they are hiding the truth. People from cultures that give undue respect to hierarchy use lengthy convoluted sentences if the question is from a client or someone in authority, and if they are sharing bad news. If you are a client from the US, and you are working with an individual from a hierarchical culture, there are ways to address issues relating to crutch words and lengthy sentences.

Be patient with people from other cultures. If you show impatience or annoyance, the individual's nervousness increases and you are likely to hear more crutch words and lengthier sentences.

Don't ask, "What do you mean?" Or ask them to repeat the sentence because you didn't understand what they said. This line of questioning would make them more nervous and the reply would be longer because they are trying harder to explain it to you. Most people from another country, if educated in a different language, may have fluency in English, but not the comfort level. Some have the habit of thinking in their language and translating their thoughts into English. So, patience helps.

Break down your question and ask more closed-ended questions. Answers to these questions are yes, no or other single words. Here is an example. If you want to know why the reports were late, ask politely in sequence:

- When was the report due?
- When did your team deliver the reports?
- So, was there a delay of ten days in delivering the reports?
- Was the report delayed because my staff did not give the data on time?
- Did you have technical issues?

These simple, gentle techniques are more likely to get the desired responses from the individual and help bridge the communications gap when you have to negotiate with people from hierarchical cultures.

YOUR GUIDE TO RULE IV

Ask yourself these questions:

1. Do I believe in the options I am proposing to clients?
2. Do I put myself in the client's shoes when I present options?
3. Am I willing to accept that I made a mistake?
4. Am I using commitment phrases or am I using too many crutch words?
5. Am I giving long-winded answers to questions?

CHAPTER EIGHT

RULE V.
RESPOND, DON'T REACT

WHERE ARE WE?

Rule IV was about speaking with conviction in negotiations when you believed in what you were saying. Rule V in this chapter deals with ways to respond to people keeping the goal of long-term relationships and results in mind. Most negotiations take a turn for the worse when people let emotions get the better of them and react in anger to others (see Figure 11).

Rule V is about maintaining your emotional equilibrium so you can make better decisions and preserve relationships. Although the rule applies to every part of a negotiation, this

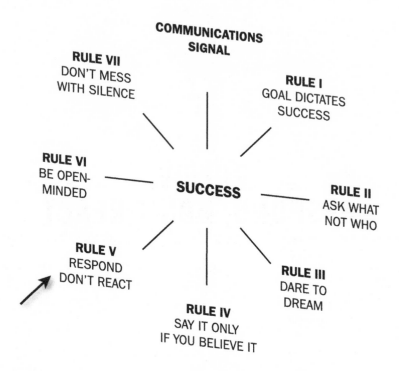

FIGURE 11. Rule V: The *Chakra* of Negotiation Principles.

ELEMENTS OF RULE V

- Anger Clouds Your Vision
- Neutralize the Situation
- Challenge to Expertise
- Defensive or Defending

chapter discusses two common types of comments that are likely to get people riled up: comments about *competitors* and comments that appear to be challenging someone's *competence*. There are ways to keep your cool in both situations when you're feeling hot under the collar.

ANGER CLOUDS YOUR VISION

Anger makes a person lose sight of the goal. A sensitive subject such as the competition can disrupt the negotiator's concentration from the goal. There is no place in the business world where people don't face the challenges of competition. Most people react when clients raise the subject of the competition.

A vendor presented a proposal to a client who kept adding more features to a project. The client was not happy with the revised pricing in the proposal. She was facing challenges in her budget from her management. The discussion became contentious. Here's how the heated argument happened:

Vendor: "We will accommodate your changes. However, we have to extend deadlines, and the changes would double your billable hours."

Client: "What? We need the reports earlier. You know, ABC Inc. (vendor's competitor) submitted a proposal. They can do it within our original timeline, and their price is a lot less."

Vendor: A junior member from the vendor team shot back,
"Did you read yesterday's paper about ABC Inc.—
nasty press? Do you think they will be around to finish
the project?"

Other members of the vendor team chimed in, "ABC Inc.
has a history of low-balling and then jacking up the price
the following year."

The manager from the vendor team intervened and neutralized the situation.

What happened in this situation is an illustration of an angry reaction to the subject of competition. The vendor team was angry. They were reacting, not responding. This reaction did not help their proposal, since some of the members in the vendor team lost sight of the goal. Had the manager not intervened, the vendor team would have lost their credibility by continuing to speak ill of their competition.

There is a difference between reacting and responding to sensitive topics. A reaction is an expression of a person's emotions, and anger tops the list of negative emotions. A response is a mature way of addressing the person while keeping the goal and relationship in mind. Eastern philosophy shows the connection between ego, anger, and reaction.

Some members of the vendor team were offended by the client's remarks about the competition. Their thoughts, "How dare they bring up ABC? We are better than ABC, and we have to prove to our client that we are better by showing that ABC does not have a good track record." A hurt ego leads to anger, which shuts down the person's discriminating power—that is, the power to distinguish between what is beneficial and what is harmful to achieving the goal and maintaining the business relationship. The desire to win an argument clouds a person's judgment. Ego is at play, and the person is ready to sacrifice success for a quick win. Before the junior member of the vendor team impulsively blurted out an answer, he should have tried to understand the reason behind the client's comments. Nothing good comes out of discrediting someone else in negotiations.

She was throwing bait, and the vendor went for it by reacting. The vendor team would have been wise to remember that the client is not out to get them. She's not doing it to be mean or petty. She wants to work with the vendor, and she is trying to bring down the pricing so she can work with them. She's just using an ineffective method to do that. If she didn't want to work with them, she would not be sitting at the negotiation table. She would have signed the deal with the vendor's competitor. Anger clouded the vendor's judgment and reasoning power. The client wants to work with the vendor, but budget parameters are limiting her, and the vendor has to make it possible for the client to work with them.

Anger is a reaction to the other person's words or deeds. All you are receiving is data, and all you can do is react. Going back to The Communications Signal, data in this case is the client bringing up the competition. It represents the red light on the traffic signal, which is a one-sided telling with no message. You don't know why the client is bringing up the competition. When you see a red light, *stop*. It is a perfect time to examine the reasons for the client's comments. Ask the questions:

- Why did my client bring up the topic of competition during negotiations?
- Why did she reach out to ABC, our major threat in the market?
- Why did she claim that ABC has promised to meet the demands?
- Why did she mention pricing?
- Why is she under budget constraints? Can we relieve this pressure?
- Can we afford to let a competitor in at this point?

When you take things personally, you react, and you are defensive. You are not giving any thought to who is asking and why. A better way is to focus on your goal.

NEUTRALIZE THE SITUATION

Be contemplative in negotiations. You don't have to answer questions immediately. A short pause and a little silence go a long way to yield better results.

Daniel learned this the hard way after making several marketing presentations to senior executives. He had to present market share results to the management of four business units. The market share had dropped for all units. One of the four business units experienced the biggest drop in share. Eric, the vice president in charge of this unit, objected to the market share numbers reported by Daniel, who reacted. He turned to the slide that showed the "customer win-loss" statistics provided by each division. He explained, "Eric, this is the data provided by your staff." It showed that among the four units in the company, Eric's business unit had experienced the highest turnover or loss of customers. It was humiliating for Eric in the presence of his peers and Daniel lost a big supporter of market research. In presentations after that, Daniel paused for thirty seconds, and then gently walked the audience through the data so they discovered the facts, or asked them a sequence of questions that led them to the truth.

When a client brings up a challenge or a sensitive topic in negotiations, pause and ask yourself:

- Why did they make the comment?
- Are they experiencing some difficulties?
- What can I say to neutralize the situation?
- What is my next move? Will it benefit both of us?
- How can I keep my focus on the goal?

Looking back at the negotiation meeting where the client brought up the subject of the competition, the manager from the vendor team had to neutralize the situation before it became a full-blown conflict. The vendor had two options—indirect or direct response.

Indirect response. Ignore the client's comment about the competition. Show a little appreciation of the client and then seek their opinion. "We have been working together for a long time, and I value our relationship. Maybe I have not thought of all possibilities here. Your input will help. Can you share with me your comments on my revised cost estimates? I welcome your suggestions for lowering the costs."

What is the strategy here? One, you are not mentioning the competition at all. Next, you are showing respect for the client's input. Last but not least, the client may share a few ideas from the competitor's proposal without revealing the source.

Direct response. You can address the competition issue, talk positively about your relationship with the client and state your interest in working on the project. "We understand your budget and timeline pressure, and we will be more than glad to work with you. Yes, ABC Inc. can handle your project, but there will be a learning curve for them. It may be worthwhile to consider how long we have worked with you on this project. We deliver accurate reports on time and within your budget. I know we are your first choice and we would like to work with you on this project. We can discuss the terms further..."

Not only does this response neutralize the situation, but it also places the vendor in a consulting role helping the client to think about the vendor's track record and the learning curve of the competition.

When you neutralize a situation, you are de-escalating a heated discussion on such a sensitive or volatile topic as your competition, and bringing the focus back to the problem and solution. In negotiations, the ability to neutralize a situation is essential for accomplishing the goal.

CHALLENGE TO EXPERTISE

How do people handle perceived challenges to their expertise and competence? Here is how an analyst with an advanced degree in statistics reacted to challenges.

The company's senior management engaged a business consultant to make improvements in customer service operations because customer satisfaction was at an all-time low. It was the role of the consultant to negotiate an agreement with the operations managers on improvements. The change could impact staffing and that made all managers anxious and irritable.

The analyst's experience during his presentation to the managers is similar to the path of The Communications Signal from data to the common understanding of the problem. The steps in the journey are:

1. Data > Information > Intelligence
2. Insights > Shared Insights
3. Common Understanding > Negotiation

DATA AND INFORMATION STAGE

The consultant accompanied the research analyst who was presenting results of a customer satisfaction study to the operations managers. The results were damaging, especially the satisfaction levels pertaining to the handling of customer service calls. The data was the customer satisfaction ratings and the information was the reason for the poor ratings. Customers were unhappy because they experienced difficulties in reaching customer service agents, lengthy hold times, dropped calls, and poor resolution of problems. Some of the customer comments included, "We kept getting transferred, sometimes the calls got cut, we were put on hold so many times, we waited so long, and finally, the agents did not solve our problems."

Senior management was not happy, so it was a touchy subject for the operations managers, who raised several objections to the research. As the bearer of bad news, the research analyst suffered the brunt of their frustration.

The audience was reacting to both the data and the information of poor ratings and the reasons for the poor ratings. The challenges from the operations managers poured in relentlessly. "Your sample is not large enough. Who is in the sample? How did you select them? Your questions are all wrong." One director of customer service produced an internal metrics report on customer calls that showed that hold times were sub-stantially lower than those reflected in the customer feedback.

The analyst who was presenting the results was fuming and he reacted to the audience. He shot back, "I have a Ph.D. in Statistics, and I have been doing market research for ten years. There is nothing wrong with the results. You need to examine customer service. The customer is always right. Your staff approved the questionnaire. We surveyed active customers, and I can guarantee the accuracy of the results. The sample is representative of all customers." He left the audience gasping, confused, and frustrated.

The business consultant saw the making of war in the room, since the analyst took the comments personally and was becoming defensive. He was reacting and not respond-ing to support the results. The audience was not interested in discrediting the research; they worried about senior man-agement's anger and the impact on their bonus checks and potential layoffs. The analyst did not see their pain. The audience reactions occupied his mind and he could only see unfavorable intentions behind their anger. His ego was hurt, and he thought they were challenging his skills and expertise.

INTELLIGENCE STAGE—
VALIDATING THE INFORMATION

The research analyst's boss, Christine, swiftly got up to neu-tralize the situation and addressed the audience, some of whom she knew personally. "Guys, you are the operations experts. I can understand your frustration since the results are alarming. There is a big difference between the data reported by our customer research, and the customer call metrics reports generated by your systems. I agree that we may not understand your definitions of dropped calls and hold times. But customers are frustrated with the calls they make to our customer service line. Let us examine how long it takes customers to reach the right customer service representative that can answer their specific questions. Help us. How best could we have asked the question? Can we make a test call to our customer service line here in your presence? It would help us re-word the surveys appropriately. Does anyone have the number for our customer service desk?"

INSIGHTS AND SHARED INSIGHTS STAGE

The audience called out ten different 1-800 numbers—one for every division and product in the company. The managers then realized the problem and acknowledged, "Hey, this may be the reason. We are giving out too many numbers to our customers. We confuse them." The intelligence is helping the audience draw conclusions, and they tried to reach a consensus.

The test calls took an average of six minutes before the right customer service agent picked up. Why? Because they had multiple customer service numbers—one for each product line—and incoming calls were forwarded several times before reaching the right agent. Some calls were dropped, and some went to the central operator, or shall we say the

Black Hole! Internal reports measured call-wait time from the moment the customer reached the correct product line to the moment an agent answered with a customary greeting. The customer's clock started the moment he or she picked up the phone. When a customer is transferred several times and put on hold a few times, six minutes may seem like sixty minutes. The internal metrics did not take into account dropped calls, transfers, and hold times caused by the multiple 1-800 numbers given out to customers.

COMMON UNDERSTANDING STAGE

The calls convinced the audience they had created the problem by giving out multiple customer service numbers. There was dead silence until one manager asked, "Hey, Christine, what now?" They had reached a common understanding of the problem. The audience accepted research results and were ready to look at solutions. The consultant thanked the managers for their understanding and asked for their consensus. "Do we all agree that we need to give one telephone number to customers?" The audience was unanimous in their agreement. One manager thanked the analyst for his research. The analyst said, "It is my job. I am sorry I overreacted."

NEGOTIATION BEGINS

The consultant then asked their permission to present two options to solve the customer service issues. Now, the operations managers began their negotiation with the consultant.

The research analyst learned a valuable lesson: his goal was to provide data to support productive discussion in the negotiation. If his data raised questions or caused pain to the audience, his role was to handle the objections with understanding, and not take it personally and turn the attention to his competency. It is not a battle of wits, which is what happens in many negotiations.

DEFENSIVE OR DEFENDING

There is a difference between being on the defensive and objectively defending or supporting the results for the benefit of the audience. Most people do not make the distinction. Being on the defensive means you are taking comments personally, going on an attack or in shield mode. Putting up arguments to show your strength—flexing your muscles—leads to a duel of egos. You are using terms like, "my research, my ideas, my expertise," forgetting that your work would have no meaning if it did not support your internal or external clients. Nothing good comes out of defensive behaviors. Go for a constructive way of promoting your idea or options.

Unlike the analyst, Christine's interest was not to prove her research right, nor did she imagine any evil intentions by the audience. She found a way to defend, that is, to support the findings of the customer satisfaction research study. Her goal was to help the audience come to a clear understanding of the message so they could take action and she achieved it. She was dealing with real people, not the brick and mortar of corporate structure. Who was in the audience? These were her colleagues she saw in the corridors, who went with her for lunch to share their trials and tribulations, and who attended meetings with her. Some empathy helps.

Most negotiations take a turn for the worse when people feel attacked and get on the defensive. Both sides in a negotiation should watch what they say and how they say it so that discussions do not become hostile. You are defensive when you take comments personally and react—I am a research expert, and I don't go wrong with the sampling methodology. I am the website designer, my designs are good, and I know what you need, how dare you question my competency—attitudes that would escalate a situation rapidly to conflict mode.

Here is another example of what you say can put people on the defensive. Randy had the habit of asking, "What do you mean?" frequently during discussions. It rattled some people. They would go into a flurry of attacks, explanations, or personal justifications. People's reactions to Randy's question were not pleasant.

"Randy, you were not paying attention. Others understood."

"Randy, I always give clear explanations. I majored in communications."

"What do you mean?" sounds accusatory and places the onus of the conversation on one person. The "you" in the question bears the burden of explanation, whereas communication is a two-way street to reach a common understanding. The better question is, "I did not understand what you said. Could you please explain?" Randy is now taking partial ownership of this conversation. It is critical for everyone in negotiation to avoid phrases that put people on the defensive.

In a negotiation, it is best to steer clear of personal remarks about people, departments, other vendors, and competition. Focus on the "what, why, how, and when," questions associated with the goal, and not on the who. Don't let the noise of others' opinions or comments drown out your purpose.

YOUR GUIDE TO RULE V

Ask yourself these questions:

1. How do I respond to such sensitive topics as competition?
2. Why is the client bringing up the competition? What does the client need?
3. How can I neutralize a situation that gives rise to conflicts?
4. How can I defend my work objectively without being defensive?
5. Would hitting the pause button help create a calming effect?

CHAPTER NINE

RULE VI.
BE OPEN-MINDED

WHERE ARE WE?

Once people learn the art of responding to others, without reacting to their comments, cultivating open-mindedness in negotiations will pave the way for strengthening relationships and results. This brings us to Rule VI, *Be Open-Minded* (see Figure 12).

Technically, this should be Rule I. However, it is better to expand your thinking with the preceding five rules and come to the sixth with an open mind—the key to success in negotiations. This chapter explains how to recognize signs of ego and closed-mindedness in others, and find ways to help them

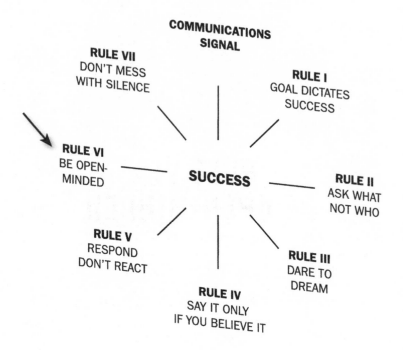

FIGURE 12. Rule VI: The *Chakra* of Negotiation Principles.

ELEMENTS OF RULE VI

- The Cost of a Closed Mind
- Ego Builds Walls, Not Bridges
- Speak Audience Language
- Inspire Open-Mindedness

keep their minds open, even when you are presenting information they don't want to hear.

THE COST OF A CLOSED MIND

When assumptions and suspicions cloud people's minds, they are not negotiating. They are bargaining. The following case is evidence of the relationship between a closed-mind and bargaining.

The product team of a financial services company was in a project planning and negotiation meeting with a marketing vendor. Jeff, the director of the product team, gave the vendor objectives for a new top priority project and discussed the challenges the company was facing in the market. Nina, who was the account specialist in the vendor's firm, came up with a scope and plan for the project in the meeting. Even though she had twenty years of experience in the industry, Jeff thought, "How could she come up with such an elaborate plan in one meeting? Why is it so expensive? Could it possibly be their way of making money, by recommending a top-of-the-line project plan, and not the features I wanted in the project? She has a hidden agenda!" Jeff saw intentions. His style of questioning showed his suspicions. He bargained Nina down to a price he had in mind at the outset. The outcome: the vendor delivered a project that raised many questions and complaints from management. Jeff may have saved $25,000, but the project did not meet company goals.

Jeff prided himself on being a tough negotiator and for keeping within budget guidelines. His closed mind, cluttered with preconceived notions about marketing vendors, created a wall between many vendors and his department and killed any creativity among the vendors, because they kept to the budget and delivered what he wanted, rather than what Jeff's company needed.

Preconceived notions, assumptions, and suspicions are biases that clutter a mind and make it closed. How do you know if a person is closed-minded? If they keep repeating their wants, raising their objections, and reacting to every comment you make. Here are typical phrases they use:

- I know. We have tried that one before.
- Why not my approach? What if your idea fails?
- You don't want to do what I want?
- What's in it for you?
- Who is behind this—someone wants to prove me wrong?
- I know I am right.

EFFECT OF A CLOSED MIND

The Adrift Website Case Study

The role-play in the negotiations class, using the Adrift Website Case, showed the impact of a closed mind. One student, Kelly, played the role of Paula, a problematic client, to help the students understand the importance of listening with an open mind—and to show them how quickly a negotiation can get derailed when people are closed-minded.

Here's how it went when Kelly played Paula, the closed-minded client, in one class. Kelly was a client service specialist in her company, and she knew how to play tough.

> Vendor team: "Paula, we are excited about your website. Your content is good. We have come up with a proposal that will help you accomplish your goal. We..."
>
> Paula cut them off: "OK, so you will not do what I want? Are you going to add the new pages? How about the logo? I did not ask for a new proposal. Is this a way to charge me more? Are you trying to cut your costs?"

Paula showed them what happens when the mind is not open to ideas. As a closed-minded client, Paula concluded that they didn't want to do what she wanted, and they had come up with something that would shortchange her. One member of the vendor team in the role-play got upset. Paula's outburst goaded him.

> "Well, Paula, if we do what you want, it will cost you fifteen thousand dollars more, and it will take an added four weeks."

A pause or silence would have been a better response to Paula's outburst.

Paula's reaction to the outburst: "So, this proposal now has
a higher price tag, and you are not doing what I want? I think
you are using this as an opportunity to jack up the price."

The vendor team was gasping and did not see a way out. *A
closed mind builds walls, not bridges!* In the role-play, by focusing on what she wanted, Kelly, playing the role of Paula, shut
the opening for any new ideas for Adrift's website. The vendor's reaction, in the role-play, was more food for a closed
mind. By referring to Paula's demands and costs, they gave
her the impression that her suspicions were right.

The team regrouped and came up with a response and
not a reaction. The vendor team discussed at length and
responded, "Paula, we understand your concerns, and our
focus is your success. Let us quickly walk you through a
similar project we did for a public speaker like you. We are
suggesting similar features for your website. These features
will address your needs and achieve your goals by leveraging
your strengths, and it is within your budget guidelines. Let
us show you. What do you think? If this idea appeals to you,
then we can discuss the details."

The tone was sincere. It conveyed an unspoken message:
"Paula, we have no hidden agendas, and we care about your
goals and needs. We helped another good public speaker succeed and would love to use that experience for your success,
too." Kelly, playing the role of Paula, smiled and accepted
the proposal.

EGO BUILDS WALLS, NOT BRIDGES

Dev accepted a job as the director of the banking practice in a services company. He managed sales, product implementation, and support for banking clients of the company. He was proud of his accomplishments at his former employer. The new employer recommended executive coaching for Dev since he was new to the company. He had been with the company for three months. During the third coaching session, when the executive coach asked him about his job, he said, "I am overworked. I have to do everything. My staff is incompetent. The sales managers make commitments to clients they cannot keep. The product implementation managers don't have clear plans. I redid the plans. The managers for the support staff are too lazy. They come in at 9:00 a.m. and leave promptly at 5:00 p.m. I changed their work hours. I don't know how they all survived in their jobs, and how they all received excellent performance ratings from my predecessor."

Dev, who was always on time, arrived late for the fifth coaching session. The executive coach asked him, "Dev, what happened?" Dev complained, "My wife hired a carpenter. This morning I saw him do the tile work in the kitchen. He didn't know what he was doing. I cannot believe that he came highly recommended by our neighbors. What is wrong with the neighbors? I fired the carpenter and started the work myself. I didn't go to work today. I cannot trust anybody. How do I handle these problems?"

The executive coach said, "Dev, do you see a pattern here?" He was puzzled. She said, "I will step out to make a phone call. While I am gone, can you go inward and think about the problems you appear to be having with the people that work for you, both at work and at home? What is the common denominator?"

When the coach returned, Dev said, "I am the common denominator. My ego is the problem. I think I am perfect. When I look at people from my perfect eyes, everyone falls short."

The coach said, "You know the problem. It is now easy to fix." Dev agreed, "I have to apologize to everyone, starting with my wife."

The coach said very gently, "Dev, when you find fault with everyone working for you, and you spend time doing their work, you are not only disempowering them, you may be failing to do your job."

It is difficult to discuss the signs of a closed mind without addressing the inflated ego, which builds an invisible wall between you and the other. Ego creates a separation—you vs. your client. It puts you on a competitive scale where you wish to make the other person lose so you can win. Your want is more critical than the other person's desires.

What are the signs of an inflated ego? When someone focuses on himself to the exclusion of others around him, and when he assumes that he can see things more clearly than others.

Focusing on yourself. You stop listening to those around you. You are busy preparing your answer in your mind when the other person has not even finished asking the question. You are also making some assumptions about what the other person is saying or going to say. You think you are right. Ego clouds judgment—the power to discriminate between what is right and what is mine. Humility is the first step toward building relationships—it comes from the acceptance you can learn from others, and everyone at the negotiation table has a vital role to play. Humility is a foundational brick for open-mindedness.

Assuming you see things more clearly. You do not know what the person sitting across the table is thinking about your project recommendations, even if she happens to be a colleague you have known for five years. You think you do, but that is a figment of your imagination. It brings to mind the ancient Indian concept of perception, *màyà*, which is a trick of the human mind. Whenever the intellect does not understand something correctly, it projects its interpretations. You conclude, "I have known her for five years and we get along very well. She will be in favor of my proposal and support my recommendations." If your colleague does not support your recommendations, you get disappointed and blame her for backstabbing you. It never crosses your mind that she is not responsible for your assumptions.

People see things the way they want to see them or how it is convenient for them. The caution here is to acknowledge your limitation to see things as they are. The path to understanding comes in handy. Pause, listen with an open mind, examine what you are seeing or hearing, clarify your doubts, and think and validate before you draw any conclusions or take any action.

Ego can stand in the way of negotiations and interfere with building relationships, since it will close your mind to other ideas and options to solve the business problem. Paula benefited from the vendor's unique proposal because she was open to their recommendations.

SPEAK AUDIENCE LANGUAGE

Listening with an open mind is essential for negotiations. One way to make your audience listen to you with an open mind is to speak in their language. I am not referring to learning to speak French because your audience is from France. What I mean is to adjust the way you speak to appeal to their interests. Companies organize themselves by functional divisions or by working styles. What appeals to employees will vary based on their jobs in corporate divisions such as marketing, finance, operations, and executive suite, or their working styles.

ADJUSTING YOUR LANGUAGE TO MATCH CORPORATE DIVISIONS

Corporate minds are more open to listening if they hear the message in a manner that appeals to them. For instance, if you are in marketing, you are more open to listening if you

FIGURE 13. Segments of Corporate Audience.

see a visual representation of a technical idea. People like to hear information and options in the language with which they are comfortable. I worked with four main categories or functional divisions of professionals in corporate America: finance, sales and marketing, operations and IT, and executive (see Figure 13). The following examples for each of the four categories explain what influences would close or open the minds of your business audience.

The Numbers Game: Speak the Language of Finance
One of the product specialists in a healthcare company presented to the managers in the sales and finance divisions a

brilliant idea to stop declining market share. She started by describing the new product idea with exciting visuals and a demo.

The manager of finance said, "Great idea! How much is this going to cost me?" When the audience from sales welcomed the idea, the finance manager's uneasiness was visible. If you are a veteran of finance, that lens colors your listening. Sales appreciated the product because they knew what their clients needed and anything that fulfilled this need meant more new deals. They were excited and their questions related to how to market the new product. The product manager spoke their language.

Finance turned pale because the new product idea meant more demands for money. The finance manager's thoughts, "Why invest money in new products or sales, if we are losing share? Shouldn't we think about cutting the budget or laying off these salespeople? If they are not bringing in the bucks, why keep them? I am sure the sales division is giving excuses for poor sales, and this fancy product idea is an outcome of their excuses." Finance's mind closed when they heard the phrase "declining market share," and they stopped hearing anything else. Finance loves hearing about declining market share—it gives them reasons to cut the budget. They understand numbers best and respond rather than react when they hear facts and figures. They are in their comfort zone.

The product specialist learned valuable lessons. First, not to give such concept presentations to both sales and finance at the same time. What opens one person's mind closes the other's mind. Next, when presenting to finance, start with sales projections for the new product, timeline, budget needed, and how soon they would be able to break even on costs and recover share they lost to the competition, and what would be the cost of not introducing the product, all backed by solid numbers from quantitative research. Now, finance would negotiate. Finance rarely gets excited about new products.

Ideas: Speak the Language of Sales and Marketing

When you present to sales and marketing professionals, put your graphics team to work. Give each graph a new exciting title, add some bright colors and diagrams, and highlight the message. Talk ideas, concepts, and message. Sales and marketing teams are more comfortable with messages that come in the form of graphics—these open doors to their thinking. Facts, figures, and processes don't grab their attention. Salespeople like to hear how easy it would be to sell the product, how to beat the competition, and how marketing could support their sales. Start with a positive message about your company and something not so right about the competition. It opens up their minds to listen to bad news you may have to deliver later on in the presentation. It's true! Try starting a talk with numbers to show declining market share.

Logistics: Speak the Language of IT and Operations

The director of communications discussed a marketing campaign with IT and operations. She was excited about the message and strategies for each market. To her astonishment, the audience sat through the entire pitch with stony silence. Then the directors of IT and operations asked, "Okay, what do you want from us? We need the logistics—where, when, how, and what." The next slide got the entire team all excited because she titled it, Logistics, and showed the timelines and resources needed. Structured thinking. The head of operations was a good friend of the director of communications and told her later, "You know, if you had started with the timeline slide, we could have understood the campaign stuff better." The director of communications thought, "After dollars and hours I spent on the sales pitch for the campaign, he calls it *stuff*!"

Laser-Sharp Focus: Speak the Language of the C-Suite

The president of a mid-sized company asked me to submit a proposal to do change management training. He was from a manufacturing background. I prepared for a tough sales negotiation. He saw in my hand a bound copy of my proposal along with a laptop set up for a presentation, and he asked me, "How long is your pitch? Would your training be able to convince my engineering team of seasoned professionals to accept a change in their processes for improved efficiency? Your bio shows you have been in the business world for less than ten years and you have zero manufacturing background. In fifty words or fewer, show me how you can do it."

Heck, my two days of preparation went down the drain. But I would not shut my mind and force a presentation on the company's president. I looked at him and said, "My training partner is a mechanical engineer with twenty years' experience in quality management. I bring you the combined strength of an experienced engineer and a certified trainer with solid business experience. Here's his bio. Do you want to meet him?" My response was less than fifty words! I focused on the president's need and concern. He accepted my proposal without meeting with the engineer, and we did the training.

Executives are results-driven. Negotiations with senior executives have to be laser-sharp and focus on the issues that concern them. Open your mind to their primary concerns. Start with your key message and build a story around it. Don't start with the details and slowly get around to your message.

Know your audience. Create a message that will resonate with the audience. You will succeed.

MATCH YOUR LANGUAGE TO DIFFERENT WORKING STYLES

The corporate audience can also be sliced a little differently (see Figure 14).

While working with cross-functional teams in change management in corporate America, I came across four interesting

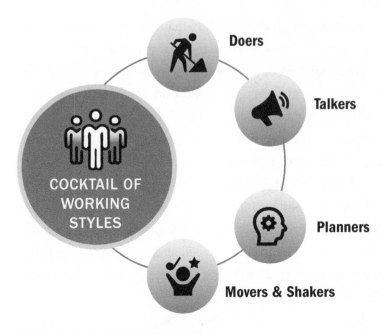

FIGURE 14. A Cocktail of Working Styles.

categories of people namely, *planners, doers, talkers,* and *movers-shakers,* each with their own working style.

The planners like to get organized and do projects in the right manner, while the movers-shakers focus on speed of action and change. They are not happy with the status quo. The doers wait till the planners put in the structure and then work rapidly to get things done. They focus on accomplishments and recognition. Talkers like to keep everyone in the loop and spread the word about accomplishments.

Chaos happened when planners had to be doers, and when movers-shakers had to develop a plan for their ideas, and talkers had to work on a project by themselves. In a large-scale project, it took all kinds to get the work done. However, when the time for discussion and negotiation came, each had a unique style. They did not speak each other's language.

Planners interacted with movers-shakers, doers, and talkers.

Planners. Dave was an extremely organized person who needed a process map before he agreed to undertake a project. He was in operations and frequently worked with folks in marketing to implement their new product ideas. The director of marketing was a mover-shaker who had a reputation for launching successful new initiatives. He was not one for details, but he knew how to get the buy-in for his ideas from senior executives. Dave was at a junior level, but he knew how to pin down the marketing director for details, and the marketing director needed Dave to implement his ideas.

Dave had to negotiate with this mover-shaker on his new initiative. He scheduled a brief telephone chat with the director of marketing, and started his pitch. "This project will be a success story like others. But it is on an aggressive timeline. My team will support you as they did on other projects. I am prioritizing projects and will put your project on the top priority list if I can get a few details from you today." The marketing director is now open to Dave's request because he knows even though he is a mover-shaker, he has to compete for the operations department's time and resources.

Doers. Dave, the planner, then has to translate the details into tasks for the people who have to do the work. It is a cascading process, and he has to negotiate with different departments to work out the scope, due dates, vacations, and other aspects involved in project management. Frequently, the doers approach planners with the phrase: "What do you want me to do first? You are changing priorities, and if you want me to do task A, then I cannot handle other tasks." It is a challenge for a mover-shaker to talk directly to a doer. A mover-shaker does not know how to translate his idea to tasks, and then he wonders why no one did his work or why the project failed.

Talkers. They link the team with the rest of the departments in the company. The talker's emails, calls, presentations, and meetings keep everyone in the loop. They serve as the mediators in negotiations between movers-shakers, planners, and doers. You cannot drag them down with details, but if you need your project to gain visibility, give them the highlights and explain the critical role they play in the project. They can get involved in every stage of a project starting from idea to final presentation of the project to management, clients, and other key stakeholders in the company.

If you are negotiating, know your audience and how they receive messages and what they are capable and willing to do with the information. Negotiations fail if you are targeting the wrong audience. A doer is rarely a decision-maker and will always say, "Let me discuss this with my manager and get back to you."

So, in negotiations for project implementation, you need a mover-shaker and a planner. Left alone, the former will make commitments the latter cannot keep. Can you send a planner alone? No, because you will hear phrases like, "No, that will take time, because...and it will cost money. We don't have staff resources." Talkers serve as good mediators because they can bridge the language gaps.

WORK-STYLE ASSESSMENT TOOL

You will see a survey titled "Team Matrix—Work-Style Assessment Tool" in the Appendix that will help you identify your work-style category.

INSPIRE OPEN-MINDEDNESS

When you are in negotiations with closed-minded people, it is best not to present conclusions or final options. Instead, walk them through the journey of discovering the possibilities. Here are a few situations where employees have to present unwelcome or unpleasant information in a meeting to management, clients, or anyone in authority in a company:

- Quarterly sales reports, when sales are on the decline.
- Project update, when you expect delays in deliverables.
- Pricing increase announcements to clients.
- Loss of business to emerging competitors.

These become harder when the audience is waiting for good news, and the mind is closed to receiving unpleasant information. It is tempting to tell the audience what they want to hear, especially if they are at a senior level in the company.

A marketing manager faced the dilemma of presenting information that contradicted a decision-maker's new product strategy. The decision-maker, Hank, was the vice president of one of the most profitable divisions in the company and wanted to move in a new strategic direction. He spent months researching the idea and then worked on selling it to executives and getting their buy-in. But, one of the senior executives agreed to vote for the idea on the condition that Hank collected valid data on the competition.

Stan headed the unit that gathered and analyzed competitive data for the company. Hank sought Stan's help to give competitive intelligence that would support his new strategic direction. That made Stan uncomfortable since Hank's mind was closed to getting data that might prove him wrong. Stan's approach was not about proving or disproving someone's ideas, and he never started with preconceived notions and biases. He generally let the results speak to him—his unique approach was to organize the data in a way so that patterns arose to provide insights about competition. Unfortunately, the intelligence did not support the division's new product strategy.

Now, came the dilemma. Stan presented the results to his boss who was the head of his division. She agreed with his conclusions and advised, "Stan, when you present this to Hank (the vice president of the product division proposing the new strategic direction), don't start with the conclusion. That will close his mind and cloud his judgment. Walk him through the patterning and thought process. Conclusions are so obvious that it would be impossible for him to miss them. Let us not share this with anyone else now."

It was a brilliant idea. Hank, the vice president, and three of his five direct reports saw the pattern. The truth stared them in the face as they came to Stan's conclusion. Although the vice president was disappointed, he was relieved he had not moved in the new strategic direction.

The lesson Stan learned from this experience: Don't tell or convey, which are one-sided conversations. Tell makes a person react and convey makes the person pause. Communicate. Make everyone part of the discussion to reach a common understanding of the problem.

You have a better chance of your options being considered favorably if the other persons in the negotiation feel they came up with the options or helped you in drafting the options. They need to be part of the solution, not just the problem.

When the mind is closed, people suspect your intentions and do not trust you. This creates a barrier in negotiations. If you are negotiating with someone who does not trust you, work on your approach to show that you have no ulterior motives or intentions. Take the case of the vice president. It was his product idea; he had spent hours developing it and getting buy-in from senior executives, and he stood to lose his credibility if the competitive analysis did not favor his idea. Stan's collaborative approach to sharing the results of his analysis cleared any suspicion the vice president might have had of Stan's intentions.

YOUR GUIDE TO RULE VI

How about this train of thought for cultivating open-mindedness in yourself and in others?

1. The client and I are here to help each other.
2. Let me not present my conclusions to closed-minded clients.
3. No one has hidden agendas.
4. Everybody adds value.
5. I need to figure out who will be at the negotiations meeting. I have to speak their language.

CHAPTER TEN

RULE VII.
DON'T MESS
WITH SILENCE

WHERE ARE WE?

This chapter is the final rule, which explains the role of silence in negotiations (see Figure 15).

Where words don't work, silence can do wonders. Silence is the language of a powerful mind.

DON'T MISUSE SILENCE

Silence is not a tool. It is not a technique to unnerve your opponent in a negotiation.

FIGURE 15. Rule VII: The *Chakra* of Negotiation Principles.

ELEMENTS OF RULE VII

- Don't Misuse Silence
- Noise in the Head Is Deafening
- Hit the Pause Button
- Silence Is Power

You are sitting with your client discussing their new projects. They want you to meet their new demands without giving you additional resources or extending the deadline. You are not willing to accept the terms, and you give them two alternatives. In one, the client has to accept your revised cost estimates for their new demands, and the second alternative requires the client to change their priorities and deadlines. The client was not happy, and they objected to the cost estimates. The client had lost a major account, and management had cut their department budgets in half. The new projects would help improve sales, and they are looking to you, their preferred vendor, to help them. You can see that their position is weak. So, you take advantage and use silence as a tool to further weaken them and make them agree to your conditions. The client is waiting nervously. You maintain your silence. The client gives in and agrees to change the priorities. You used silence to make the client give in to your terms. Such tactics do not contribute to building strong relationships.

WHEN SILENCE HELPED ACHIEVE STILLNESS

Stillness is not the same as silence. Stillness means a balanced, unwavering mind. Silence helps achieve stillness.

Beth worked for a financial services company. She was scheduled to give a market brief to the executive team at 11:00 a.m. It was an intimidating experience for most people. Just an hour before the big presentation, her boss called her to a meeting. Beth thought she wanted to give her some last-minute tips. However, that was not the case. Her boss had heard rumors that Beth had discussed transferring to another department with human resources, and it had upset her. It was a twenty-minute tirade about protocols and another ten minutes of inquiry about Beth's reasons. Beth silently listened to her and said, "Sorry." Any explanation or comments from her would have provoked more anger and prolonged the conversation. Beth did not waste time seeing any intentions in her boss's actions. Beth's silence shortened the meeting and gave her time to focus on the presentation.

Now, Beth had thirty minutes before the presentation. She went into her office, sat down, and closed her eyes. Listening to music cut out the noise in her head—her boss' sharp words—and her plan of counter-attack, possibly a call to human resources to complain, and a series of such competing thoughts. With determination, Beth turned her attention to the goal—she looked at Slide #1 to review the highlights of her presentation to the C-Suite. She then slowly walked into the executive boardroom. The executives were cross-examining the speaker who preceded her. He looked pale. Beth's turn came, and she walked straight to the podium and spoke.

The CEO (chief executive officer) asked her, "Beth, our market share is declining because we are not keeping pace with the changes in the market. What will happen to our market share next year if we don't take action now to introduce the new products? What's at stake?"

Beth told him calmly, "We stand to lose 15 percent of our base."

He looked at Beth's boss and said, "Can you facilitate an emergency strategy session with the divisions?"

Beth's boss called her later to apologize. She was not a bad person—she had just reacted to the news. It surprised her that Beth remained calm during the presentation. No one knew the turmoil in Beth's mind. She held steadfast to her goal of alerting the company about the impending loss of market share. Nothing else mattered. Being silent helped. Holding onto the goal gives you the balance you need in negotiations. Silence and contemplation take the focus away from blaming someone else for the business problem and help you identify what you did to evoke this response from others. Beth accepted that she should have approached her boss first about the transfer. Her mistake. If you know this, the solution is easy, since you control how you behave. The goal should be the anchor to create a balance in your mind.

Listening to soft music or inspirational talks, taking a walk, and reading a book are some techniques to maintain the stillness. Meditation helps. It slows your breath. If you notice, your breathing turns rapid when your emotions rise. Keeping your mind synchronized with a slow breath prevents you from reacting. It aids the steadiness of purpose.

NOISE IN THE HEAD IS DEAFENING

External sounds can cause havoc in meetings. But noise or disruptions in your mind can be deafening. Colleen, a training consultant, had just completed a three-hour webinar on conflict resolution. It was exhausting because the audience was hostile. She had to remain neutral, and that drained her.

Phew! What a relief when it was all over. However, the whole experience was playing and replaying in her mind at a feverish pace. It was about this time she received a call from Pamela, who was the training coordinator for Colleen's primary client. Pamela's call was ill-timed. She surprised Colleen with her opening statement, "Colleen, we want to expand our executive coaching capability. More people want to enroll in the coaching program for professional development. You are our best coach. We want to bring the hourly rate down by 25 percent because of our limited budget. We can probably make up by volume. We now have more coaches, and we are approaching them too."

Pamela went on. However, Colleen stopped listening because of the boom box in her head. She lost her balance because she perceived herself as a victim of foul play by Pamela, the client. The potential threat of rivalry from other coaches disturbed Colleen, and she drew hasty conclusions. Thoughts were racing in Colleen's agitated mind.

- Pamela is using sales tactics to bring my price down.

- What volume? If I am the lead executive coach, why bring my price down?
- Who are the other coaches? Why did I not know about them?
- I bet you they will not ask the other coaches to lower prices.
- I am their comfort zone—they can use familiarity to bring down my pricing.
- The clients are using me. *How dare they?*

Without a pause, Colleen replied, "Pamela, how many other coaches? Brenda never told me about them. Twenty-five percent is a drastic cut in pricing." Her reply surprised Pamela. She said, "Colleen, I did not expect this from you."

Pamela's admonition made her pause. She was silent while she was thinking, "Oh God, what did I do? My goal is to continue playing the lead role and enable the expansion of their coaching program. My hasty outburst did not support the goal."

She regretted her hastiness and told Pamela, "So sorry, Pamela. Can we schedule a call to discuss the coaching program? I have had a rough day. You are my most valuable client. How exciting that you wish to expand the coaching program. It means that our program is working. I want to give this discussion the due attention it deserves. I am available tomorrow."

Pamela said, "Colleen, what a relief. That sounds more like you."

Colleen needed silence to regain her balance. You make bad decisions when both external and internal noise disrupts your mind. Your intellect, which can discriminate between right and wrong decisions, performs better when you are in silence. Peace within is the foundation for the right decisions. Eastern philosophy talks extensively about silence, which is your true nature. Silence does not mean, "not talking" or "keeping quiet." It involves *blocking the external sounds and ignoring the noise within your mind*. Noise in your head can be deafening. It disrupts your stillness or sense of balance. It is like throwing a rock into still waters. Observing the noise within your mind distances you from it. If you react, the noise becomes louder.

The noise here does not imply sounds. It means personal and professional issues, anger and related emotions, and direct and indirect pressure from other people who have a vested interest in the outcome of your negotiation. It is mental chatter. "What will the other person think? Why is she frowning? What did I do?"

It is perhaps the reason you close your eyes and focus on the breathing and physical movement in yoga. The instructor tells you not to look at others or compete with them—no distractions, no compare and contrast, and no judgments.

HIT THE "PAUSE" BUTTON

When somebody proposes something or attacks you, you need not react immediately. Consider the attack as a message—yellow light—pause and think, and ask yourself, "Why did they say that?" You should not feel compelled to react to people. The best example of an unpleasant reaction happened in the case where a member of the vendor team spoke ill of a competitor immediately after the client mentioned the competition. One member spoke up, and that had a ripple effect, and all the members chimed in to speak against the competitor. (See Chapter 8, Rule V.)

When you have the strong urge to react, try asking yourself three questions:

1. Will it benefit me?
2. Will it benefit the other person(s)?
3. Will it benefit our goal?

If your answer is no to any of the three questions, go into silence. The pause gives steadiness, an essential ingredient for stillness. You may fail sometimes—it is tough not to give in to the noises. Use silence to give yourself or the others time to let suggestions, options, or solutions sink in.

A company had hired Tim as a leadership consultant to resolve a conflict between two team leaders, Sean and Stella. A great deal of mistrust existed between them, leading to a battle-ridden relationship. Tim met with them individually and then together. The bone of contention in the conflict was the work-at-home rules for their staff. The team leaders had to come up with a uniform policy for both teams. One team leader came up with a set of rules, and the other did not seem to like any of the rules.

Tim encountered a shouting match when he met the two leaders together. It surfaced all their old wounds and what ensued was a heated exchange. Tim was not clear if their objections related to the work-at-home policy or an even bigger question, "Was it personal?" He intervened by asking Sean and Stella to write three pros and cons of working at home, and then, for each to come up with three new rules for work-at-home guidelines. Tim took their individual notes and quietly read them and requested both team leaders to remain silent while he had time to think.

Tim's next move was to write six rules on two pieces of paper. Both papers had the same six rules. Tim wrote the rules in his own words. By now, each team leader had at least ten minutes of silence—a deliberate attempt to cut down the noise in their heads. He gave one piece of paper to each and instructed both to read it silently and circle the three rules they wanted to include in a uniform policy for work-at-home guidelines. Sean and Stella quietly returned their responses to Tim. Both chose the same three rules, but for different reasons. Their disagreements had focused on these reasons.

The three rules both chose were:

1. The staff could work at home only three days a week.
2. They had to do a full day's work.

3. They had to come in person to work on days they had management meetings.

Sean chose medical issues and commuting distance as the two reasons for allowing staff to work at home. Stella insisted on parenting as the main reason for work-at-home and commuting distance as a secondary reason. However, both wanted to be fair to everyone in their staff—a common goal. Both Stella and Sean were happy that they picked the same rules, and they realized that maintaining silence while writing down their choices helped them solve the problem. The silence cleared their minds. Sean admitted that if they had focused on the rules and not the reasons, they could have worked this out without any conflicts. Silence with less noise means more clarity for coming up with solutions.

Looking back at the conversation between Colleen and her client Pamela, had Pamela not brought up the existence of other coaches, Colleen's reaction would have been less aggressive. Competition is a hard pill to swallow for someone who regarded herself as the elite, exclusive coach. Precision in options—sticking to the point—accompanied by silence would have served Pamela better. Colleen should have hit the pause button to buy some time for digesting the news. Their mutual goal was to expand the coaching program.

Although Pamela did not go on a rant, she flooded Colleen with data, some of which took her by surprise. Presenting a 25 percent rate drop in coaching fees, while she casually mentioned new competitors, opened the door for bargaining. It does not strengthen the relationship. Can the client afford to lose a valued executive coach? Here is a modified replay of their chat that would have worked better for both.

Pamela opens the conversation, "Colleen, you have made the coaching program popular. More people want to enroll. We want to expand our executive coaching capability, but management cut our budget. What do you think? Do you have any ideas? You don't have to give me an answer right away. Do you need time to think?" Pamela remains silent.

Colleen replies, "Thanks, Pamela. I want to give it some thought. I am just recovering from a stressful training session and cannot think. Can we reschedule?" Pamela agrees.

SILENCE IS POWER

It is our natural state. Tap into it. Silence is about contemplation and giving the other person or yourself time to make the right move. When Harry returned from a lengthy international trip, he found out that one of his credit cards had charged late fees and levied interest charges for three months. He thought he had set it up online for automatic payment, but apparently, the payments didn't go through. Negotiation time!

He called the credit card company's customer service, and the customer service agent told him, "Sir, you should be happy we didn't cancel your card when you were on your trip, so you have no choice but to pay both the interest and the penalty. That's the rule." Harry shot back with complaints. There was much back and forth with no resolution. Noise. He finally asked to speak to a supervisor. The agent reluctantly connected Harry to a supervisor.

The supervisor patiently listened to Harry's tirade and responded, "Sir, I see from your history with us you are a loyal customer, and we have every intention of keeping you. I also see you have applied for a business account with us. The bank appreciates your loyalty, and I am glad to inform you we approved your business account application." She then paused for Harry, who threatened to withdraw his business application if she did not cancel the late fees and interest charges. He was all set for a good fight.

The supervisor calmly asked Harry, "Sir, what would make you happy?" He restated his request to cancel the penalties and interest charges. The supervisor said after a brief pause, "Sir, I will exercise my authority to cancel the penalties, but the interest charge is another matter. I can cancel interest for the most recent month. Would that make you happy? You don't have to answer right away. I will hold, while you think about it. I know you don't like recorded messages or music while you are holding. So, I will turn off the music and automated messages. Also, sir, it would be in your favor if we resolved the matter when you are on the call with me."

The supervisor was quiet while she let Harry think. No music, no noise, no words to persuade him. Her goal was to keep his business as a personal and business cardholder. Harry did not want to deal with a new card company, and he did some mental mathematics, and it took a few minutes for him to decide in favor of the option presented by the supervisor.

Why did he choose the option? Both the bank and Harry had a similar goal—the bank wanted to keep his business, and he wanted to maintain his account. The supervisor's calm and friendly approach made a difference. I wonder if he would have made that decision if she had tried high-pressure tactics and did not give him time to think in absolute silence.

Harry was so impressed with her approach, he asked the supervisor, "I like your approach. What's your trick? How did you get me to settle for the option in a call?" Her reply left a lasting impression on him, "There is no trick. My goal is to keep you as a satisfied customer. I know you want to remain with the bank. You and I are on the same team. I wanted you to make your own decision without regrets." Finally, she laughed and said, "My real trick is silence."

It is difficult to be silent when the client is angry. The best solution is to focus on the *goal*. Avoid talking when your client is mad because anger shuts down a person's rational thinking and open-minded listening. There would be no point in talking when someone is angry. A little silence after asking what you can do to make the client happy steers the conversation away from anger. If you think you cannot afford to make the customer happy and cancel the late fees, it is the right time for contemplation. Ask yourself, "Why is the customer angry?" The customer is not happy with something that happened. He thinks he did the right thing by setting his account on automatic payment, but the system failed on him, so he is in a bad mood. Words like "happy" change the mood and tone.

Some people may wonder about the client's interpretation of silence. What if we don't speak and the customer thinks we agreed with their demands or that we are trying to unnerve them? If you observed the six rules that precede this one, people would not misinterpret your intentions.

SILENCE HELPS RESOLVE CONFLICTS

During a meeting to discuss a communications campaign for a new product, a client raised several objections to the marketing consultant's proposal. Jack, who represented the marketing company, patiently explained the campaign for launching the client's product, "Over the course of ninety days before the launch date, my team will work to generate exposure for your product. This is accomplished by publishing articles about your company, your industry, and the product. We will leverage your customer database and conduct email campaigns, and pitch national journalists to cover your product in high-quality media outlets, and book your executives for interviews. Your product will create a stir in the market."

The client asked Jack, "How do I know your options will work? We have had very poor response in the past with email and media campaigns to small businesses. Will national journalists care about this product? Why do you have to contact three hundred national journalists? Your pricing is too high."

The marketing consultant paused. He realized that she was under budget constraints, and her main objection to his proposal was the pricing. He saw no point in addressing each objection individually. The client went on a tirade again, and asked for a revision in pricing and added some of her earlier demands. Jack let the client vent, and after a brief pause said, "Our company has had the fortune of working with you for five years to launch products. With your leadership, the products have gained considerable visibility in the small business market. I want to support you in achieving the same level of success. This new product shows promise and will create quite a stir in your market. I want you to be happy with the campaign. Can we walk through the different options in the proposal and select the ones you prefer? We will consider variations to the options. It means time to redo the options. However, you are the client, and the choice is yours. Do you want time to think about it?"

Dead silence ensued giving the client time to go inward and think, "Jack has worked with me for five years and supported me in launching products. The launches have created a stir in the small business market, and helped build our market share. His proposals have always been reasonable in pricing, and on target with the strategies. I can bring the pricing down, but it may not be good for our business relationship. I have nothing to lose by trying Jack's proposal, as is." Silence helped the client clear her mind, and listen to her inner common-sense voice.

Had Jack dwelled on every one of the client's objections, and reacted to the discussions, their talk would have taken a different direction. Jack's strategy of gently reminding the client of their past successes in marketing campaigns and the need to build market share worked. The client approved the proposal. The campaign yielded the results needed for the client to achieve the market share goal. For Jack, it was another step in the direction of a long-term relationship and results.

Silence helps if you intend to help the other person decide. Conflict is not between people. It exists in our minds based on how we perceive others. Silence helps resolve the conflict in our minds.

YOUR GUIDE TO RULE VII

Suggestions to quiet your mind before you negotiate:

1. Write the goal of the meeting.
2. Think positive—stay away from negative people.

3. A brisk walk out in the open doesn't hurt.
4. Listen to soft music.
5. Read or listen to inspirational speeches.
6. Meditation helps.

A SUCCESS STORY

Did the book address questions posed in the Opening Thoughts?

> Why do I feel like I am on a seesaw of wins and losses in my business negotiations? Even when I win, I sometimes feel like I lost something. Tools and techniques I picked up in books and training are not foreign, so what am I missing? What will put me on the path to success? What is the yardstick for success?

It did for Paula of the Adrift Website Case, which is a real success story. After being in business for ten years and experiencing many failed attempts by several website designers, she found the one designer who knew how to work with her to get what she needed, not what she wanted.

The designer met with Paula to gather data on her website, her products and services, and her dreams for business growth. He checked her website completely, read some of her articles and listened to a couple of videos. The designer even talked to one of her clients. He met with her a second time to discuss the situation. Paula wanted to increase her visibility in the corporate market for training and to stay ahead of her competition. She thought if her website had more pages on her workshops, videos, and blogs, she would gain the visibility and beat the competition. She also complained about the cost of building or revising websites.

The designer then attended one of Paula's training sessions and knew what she offered. He met with her again and both came to a common understanding of the problem—Paula's website failed to project her unique strength as a public speaker. She stood out from the rest of the trainers because she was a powerful public speaker. Unfortunately, the website made her look like the other trainers.

The website designer cruised the internet to find the names of powerful public speakers and chose the two most like Paula. He was patient with her demands and presented to her the two options with his intention to make her succeed like the other two speakers. He dared her to dream. The designer said, "Paula, you need to take photographs of yourself that show the power in you to captivate an audience.

I assure you the Home Page with your photograph and a one-minute video of your talk and keywords on your capability will establish your brand."

Paula argued, "What about all the training work I do, and the tons of articles, videos, and blogs I want to share with my audience?" The designer paused and said in a polite tone, "Paula, you have a choice. I can fulfill all your demands and make you look like the other trainers, or create a website that will make you stand out like the other two speakers. The costs for both options are the same. However, the second option is what you need to gain visibility and grow your business. Think about the options. I will wait for your decision."

The website designer lived in India. Silence was his nature. He did not react to her unreasonable demands nor did he offer anything he did not believe. He shared the options with conviction and proof, and opened her mind to ideas. He said nothing negative about past designers. He said he had an advantage over the previous designers because he had seen Paula in action as a trainer. He thanked her for the training and the opportunity to redo her website.

Paula chose the option that was based on her need, not on her desires. The website was completed in four weeks and took Paula by surprise. The designer captured the essence of her personality and her brand, on her website. Paula received several positive comments about her website from clients, and with his help, she built an email list of prospects. Paula wrote a strong recommendation for the designer and gave him the freedom to use her website as a testimonial for his work.

It was a success story because the designer did not focus on wins. He would have made the same money regardless of the options Paula chose, but by presenting a compelling case for the second option, the designer built a strong relationship and lasting results for both Paula and his business.

As a researcher and a catalyst for positive change in people, I am always interested in knowing the impact of the learnings in this book on your mind and your jobs. Reach out to me with questions, comments, or suggestions, and even better, your success stories.

TEAM MATRIX: WORK-STYLE ASSESSMENT TOOL

Referenced in Chapter Nine, Rule VI.

I developed this tool for my negotiation and team-building classes. It helps you identify your work-style category. The Table has twenty-one statements that characterize one or more of the four work styles: Doer, Planner, Talker, and Mover-Shaker. Read each statement and check the box in the column titled "True," if it characterizes your style of work. If it does not, mark it as "False." Some of the statements may characterize more than one work style category.

Tally the results to see which of the four categories is most likely to fit your work style. (Use of this tool is restricted to reader's self-assessment; any other use requires author's permission.)

	Statements	True	False	Code
1	I finish all my work on time.			D
2	I do one task at a time.			D
3	I like clear instructions for my work.			D
4	I do not like unexpected changes in projects.			D
5	I always try to exceed my goals.			D
6	I like to be recognized for my work.			D
7	I organize and prioritize my work.			P
8	I like to know goals and strategies.			P
9	I plan for contingencies.			P
10	I share information with everyone.			D, P, T
11	I have regular update meetings.			P
12	I send regular written updates.			P
13	I like to represent my team in meetings.			T
14	I keep in touch with my work contacts.			T

	Statements	True	False	Code
15	I like to talk about accomplishments.			T, MS
16	I volunteer for new assignments.			MS
17	I try new ways of doing things.			MS
18	I don't hesitate to share my ideas with management.			MS
19	I am open to listening to complaints of people.			T, MS
20	I get tired of doing repeat work—I like new challenges.			MS
21	I never say, never—I can do any work I set my mind to do.			MS

Key: D=Doer, P=Planner, T=Talker, MS=Mover-Shaker

ABOUT THE AUTHOR

Mala Subramaniam speaks from experience. From working as an analyst in a bank in New York, to middle management marketing roles with employers such as Dun & Bradstreet, IBM, GE Healthcare Technology, and Horizon Blue Cross Blue Shield of New Jersey, she has negotiated with a cross section of people all the way up to the C-Suite to accomplish strategic and transformational projects. Mala's talks on cross-cultural communications, leadership training, and executive coaching programs have reached many clients since 2006, including Cognizant Technology Solutions, Express Scripts, Putnam Financial, Williams Sonoma, NASDAQ, Lincoln Financial, The Hartford Insurance, BCBS, Comcast, A3Logics and Meltwater.

Her blend of Indian philosophy and US American psychology powers this book. Her training, titled *Soft, Yet Powerful Negotiations*, helps the daily situations confronted by working professionals facing demanding clients, limited resources, and profit-driven management.

She earned her Master's in Sociology from Madras University, India, and an MBA from Rutgers University, USA. Mala is also a Dale Carnegie certified public speaker and Achieve-Global certified trainer. Visit www.beyondwins.com to learn more about Mala. Her email is mala@mktinsite.com.

Made in the USA
Las Vegas, NV
27 November 2021

35398780R00135